DATE DUE

3-2931

Jaime Escalante

TITLES IN THE
LATINO BIOGRAPHY LIBRARY SERIES:

Jaime Escalante

Inspirational Math Teacher

ANNE SCHRAFF

Enslow Publishers, Inc.
40 Industrial Road
Box 398
Berkeley Heights, NJ 07922
USA

http://www.enslow.com

Library of Congress Cataloging-in-Publication Data:

Schraff, Anne E.
   Jaime Escalante : inspirational math teacher / Anne Schraff.
      p. cm.
   Includes bibliographical references and index.
   Summary: "Explores the life of math teacher Jaime Escalante, including his childhood in Bolivia, his road to teaching in the United States, and the innovative teaching techniques that made him an inspiration to his students"—Provided by publisher.
   ISBN-13: 978-0-7660-2967-5
   ISBN-10: 0-7660-2967-0
   1. Escalante, Jaime—Juvenile literature. 2. Mathematics teachers—California—Biography—Juvenile literature. 3. Hispanic American mathematics teachers—California—Biography—Juvenile literature. I. Title.
   QA29.E73S37 2009
   510.71—dc22
   [B]
                                     2008004704

Printed in the United States of America

10 9 8 7 6 5 4 3 2 1

To Our Readers: We have done our best to make sure all Internet Addresses in this book were active and appropriate when we went to press. However, the author and the publisher have no control over and assume no liability for the material available on those Internet sites or on other Web sites they may link to. Any comments or suggestions can be sent by e-mail to comments@enslow.com or to the address on the back cover.

Every effort has been made to locate all copyright holders of material used in this book. If any errors or omissions have occurred, corrections will be made in future editions of this book.

♻ Enslow Publishers, Inc., is committed to printing our books on recycled paper. The paper in every book contains 10% to 30% post-consumer waste (PCW). The cover board on the outside of each book contains 100% PCW. Our goal is to do our part to help young people and the environment too!

Illustration Credits: Courtesy of Angel Navarro, p. 98; Angelo Cavalli/Getty Images, p. 13; Courtesy of a35mmlife via Flickr™, p. 65; Associated Press, pp. 8, 86, 111; Courtesy of Dept. of Special Collections/UCLA Library, p. 83; Enslow Publishers, Inc., p. 14; Getty Images, p. 51; Herald Examiner Collection/Los Angeles Public Library, p. 68; © istockphoto.com/Danny Warren, p. 22; Courtesy of Jaime Escalante, pp. 3, 5, 19, 28, 30, 33, 38, 40, 42, 48, 72, 94; Courtesy of Karl Swinehart via Flickr™, pp. 24; Public domain image via Wikipedia.org, p. 54; Courtesy Ronald Reagan Library, p. 103; Shutterstock/Danny Warren, p. 44; Shutterstock/Mark Breck, p. 9; Courtesy of Stormwind via Flickr™, p. 60; Photo by Tim McGarry via Flickr™ of mural by Hector Ponce (www.hectorponce.com), p. 100; © Warner Brothers/Everett Collection, p. 105; Warner Bros./Photofest, p. 110.

Cover Illustration: Courtesy of Jaime Escalante.

Contents

1

Starting Over

The stocky, square-jawed thirty-three-year-old man had arrived in the United States from Bolivia at the end of 1963. What he needed now was a job—any job. He had a wife and young son to support. He spoke almost no English. He had memorized a few English words to help him in asking for a job. His brother-in-law drove him to car washes and restaurants where he asked if they needed anybody.

For the past decade, Jaime Escalante had been a science and mathematics teacher. He was a dynamic and brilliant teacher. His delightful sense of humor endeared him to his students. Several schools in Bolivia were vying for his services. He tutored students privately, too, and there was not enough time for all who wanted to study with him. Now, he was just another immigrant looking for work.

Shortly before Jaime Escalante left Bolivia, he saw much unrest in his country. Here, men carry an injured friend after he was shot in a clash with rival demonstrators in La Paz, Bolivia, on October 26, 1962.

Escalante and his wife had decided to come to the United States for a better future for themselves and their son. Teachers in Bolivia, even excellent ones like Escalante, were poorly paid. There was ongoing economic and political unrest in the country. It seemed the right time to go north.

Escalante was alone in the United States except for his wife's relatives. His wife and son remained in Bolivia awaiting word that he had a job and a place to live.

Pasadena's History

The old California Rancho San Pasqual was one of the large land grants given by Spain and later Mexico to ranchers who would develop the land. San Pasqual was also an American Indian village on the San Gabriel River. In 1859, Americans bought the rancho, and in 1867, they built a ditch to bring water from a nearby stream. By 1874, hundreds of people settled on the land and a permanent name for the new town was chosen—Pasadena, which in the Chippewa Indian language means "crown of the valley." From oak tree and poppy-covered land sprang a city that became home to many Americans and immigrants to the United States.

Completed in 1927, Pasadena City Hall is on the National Register of Historic Places.

Then they would join him. Escalante lived in Pasadena, California, north of Los Angeles. On this particular day, he walked down a street in Pasadena and stopped at yet another restaurant.

The large blue Van de Kamp's restaurant was right across the street from Pasadena City College. Escalante entered the restaurant and haltingly asked for a job, using his memorized English words. The sour-faced manager looked at the man who obviously was not a teenager like many of his other employees. But he needed someone to mop the floor. He handed Escalante a mop. The mathematics teacher who had held his classes spellbound in Bolivia now had to prove to this man that he could mop a floor. Escalante swept the floor first, then mopped and scrubbed the floor until it shone. At the end of the day, he stacked chairs on top of the tables and mopped some more. The manager came over to inspect the work he had done and smiled in approval. "See you tomorrow, Jaime," he said.[2]

The next morning, Escalante was sore from lifting the heavy chairs around so he could mop the floor, and from stacking them atop tables at the end of the workday. He was hardly able to get out of bed because his muscles were not used to this kind of physical exertion. He was accustomed to a teacher's routine in which the mind was used more than the muscles. Only a few weeks

> "I have always been a person with a lot of ganas" (the will to succeed).[1]

earlier, he had been enjoying the admiration and respect of hundreds of students. He was the envy of fellow teachers who could not command a classroom like he did. But all that was in the past. Escalante was now thankful that he had a job mopping the floor of a restaurant in the United States of America.

Jaime Escalante knew he was starting over at the bottom rung of a very tall ladder. He clung fiercely to his dream of somehow becoming a teacher again. He loved that work too much to give it up forever. Even as he mopped the floor and carried dirty dishes he liked to say, "The greatest thing you have is your self image, a positive opinion of yourself. You must never let anyone take it from you."[3]

Childhood in Bolivia

Jaime Alfonso Gutierrez was born on December 31, 1930, in La Paz, Bolivia. His ethnic roots lay in the Aymara Indian people of the country. As an adult, he would say proudly, "The Aymara knew math before the Greeks and the Egyptians."[1] His parents, Zenobio and Sara Escalante, were teachers in the Aymara Indian village of Achacachi on the *altiplano*, or high plain. Jaime had an older sister, Olimpia, and eventually, there would be three more children born to the family, Bertha, Jose, and Raul.

Sara Escalante was a hardworking woman deeply interested in her children. When he became a teacher himself, Jaime Escalante was asked if there was any one person who most influenced his life. "My mom," he said. He felt she had changed the course of his life. He described a simple incident that planted the seeds of curiosity in his mind. His mother held up an orange

Jaime was descended from the Aymara Indian people. Above is an Aymara women with a llama in Bolivia.

before her small son, and said, "This is a sphere." Then she cut the orange in half and said, "This is symmetry."[2]

Sara Escalante's father, Jose Gutierrez, also played a major role in the boy's life. Gutierrez was a retired teacher and an amateur philosopher. Jaime loved to spend time with his grandfather, taking long walks and playing word games.

Zenobio Escalante, Jaime's father, was a troubled man. He had a serious alcohol problem. He became angry easily and struck his wife and children. One incident that remained in the boy's mind occurred when Jaime was eight years old. Jaime had just received a

Bolivia

Bolivia is a landlocked country with no access to the sea. It is located in South America and has an area of 424,165 square miles (1,098,581 square kilometers). Bolivia is about the size of California and Texas combined. The Andes mountains run through the country north to south. Most of Bolivia's 8 million people live on the *altiplano*, a high mountain plain. Here the beautiful Lake Titicaca, the highest navigable lake in the world, is found. Bolivia was part of the great Inca empire until 1532 when it was conquered by Spain. In 1825, Simon Bolivar drove the Spanish out and became the first president of Bolivia, which is named in his honor.

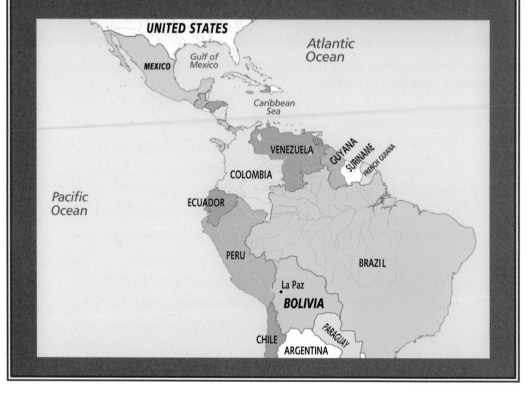

packet of gum from his friend, Armando, and he was enjoying chewing a piece when his father appeared. As he often was, Zenobio Escalante was drunk. When he saw Jaime chewing the gum, he accused the boy of stealing it. Jaime explained that the gum was from his friend, but his father refused to believe him. He slapped Jaime across the face and accused him of lying. Jaime was deeply hurt that his father could be so cruel and unfair.[3]

The Escalantes lived in a tile and adobe house with three rooms. Though both parents taught, they received low wages and had to struggle to make ends meet. The house was about one hundred yards from the village plaza where there were shops, government offices, and a church.

As a small boy, Jaime spent most of his time making up games for himself and playing in the dirt patio beside his house. He feared his father's dark moods and tried to stay out of his way as much as possible. One day, Jaime's life changed drastically. He awoke in the morning to see his mother carrying all the family possessions out to a yellow truck. The other children were already in the truck. Sara Escalante told Jaime he had to stay behind to explain to his father what had happened.

When Zenobio got home from work, Jaime told him that his wife and children had left him and moved to La Paz. Zenobio Escalante was a bitter and frustrated man. He resented the poor pay he received as a teacher and he felt hopeless about his future. When he was sober, he realized that he treated his family poorly, but he was never strong enough to overcome his drinking. Sober when he learned his family had finally grown weary of his behavior, he did the right thing for his son. He gave Jaime a bus ticket to La Paz along with directions to a house there. Then he sent Jaime on his way.

Jaime spent six hours on the bus going from Achacachi to La Paz. He carried only a few pieces of clothing tied in a bundle on his back. He walked to the address his father had given him. When he rapped on the door, his mother was there. She took Jaime in her arms and hugged him.

In the years that followed, Zenobio Escalante came for a few visits. He was not welcome because everyone in the family feared him. Neither Jaime nor the other two older children called him Papa. The family spoke of him in whispers, referring to him as "he." The whole family dreaded the sight of Zenobio Escalante coming down the path to their home.

One day, Jaime's father visited the family and he found his son reading. He taunted Jaime and told him he was holding the newspaper the wrong way. He slapped Jaime across the forehead. He was very drunk, and he called his son a cheat and a thief. He struck him hard across the left ear. Everyone was relieved when he finally left.

When Jaime started school, he was wearing the long trousers and long-sleeved shirts the Aymara children wore in Achacachi. The children at the La Paz elementary school wore short sleeves and short pants. The children laughed at Jaime, but not for long. He was very good at arithmetic and, even more importantly in the eyes of his classmates, he was very skilled at sports. He played soccer, basketball, and handball.

Although Jaime was smart, he did not always bring home a good report card. This troubled his mother. She said if he failed in school people would say of him, "This guy is not well educated," and he would not go far in life.[4]

Jaime Escalante was very restless in school. It was hard for him to sit still and listen to the teacher. He later said of himself as a schoolboy, "I was so active I couldn't stay still for more than two minutes. I was hyperactive."[5]

Sara Escalante moved with her children to a house on Graneros Street. It was a very steep street, which provided endless fun for Jaime. He was fascinated by experiments. He was becoming a young scientist. Although Jaime confided his dreams to his older sister, Olimpia, his little sister, Bertha, was his partner in many wild experiments.

> *"I had a teacher that told me, 'I'm going to teach you something that you will remember all your life—fractions.'"*[6]

Jaime was interested in engineering projects and discovering how things work. He built a wooden car to race down Graneros Street. At the wheel was Bertha. When the car tipped over, Bertha went flying into an open manhole. She went in headfirst and then slowly emerged from the sewer covered with foul-smelling slime, though unhurt.

Jaime also experimented with electricity. His scientific curiosity included a wild sense of humor. He grasped a small generator and then shook hands with Bertha who had no idea what was about to happen. To her horror she got a shock she never forgot. (This, of course, was very dangerous and could have hurt or killed his sister, though Jamie was not aware of that at the time.) Jaime liked to stand on a metal plate that sent electrical currents through him. He enjoyed having his hair stand on edge as Bertha and the other children screamed in terror.

After saving enough money, Sara Escalante moved her family again. This time she chose a home high on a western slope called Sopocachi. The new house was on a steep dirt road. Cows and sheep grazed on the scrub brush on the hillside. The Escalante dogs ran free. Jalisco, the dachshund, and a white mutt named Fifi, played daily with Jaime and the other children. The house was very simple with no modern conveniences. Later, a second story was added to provide more room.

Jaime walked to school every day. His love of math and science was growing. He was always curious about

As a child, Jaime Escalante was creative as well as mischievous. Above is Jaime at age seven.

how everything worked. He also loved adventure and was willing to try anything. Jaime was fearless. During a handball game, when the ball soared and then vanished down a drainpipe, Jaime went into action. He climbed the school wall to recover the ball. He lost his balance and went tumbling down, breaking his arm and gashing his forehead. He bore a lifelong scar on his forehead from the incident, but it did not in the least tame him.

Jaime was famous in his group of friends for his wild sense of humor and his fighting ability. Jaime did not fight in anger, but always in fun. Jaime and his friends would stage street fights among themselves, which always drew a large crowd. The strong, quick Jaime could beat almost anybody, and after the bout, everybody would be friends again. His reputation soared in Sopocachi.

A Student at San Calixto

When Jaime Escalante was fourteen, his mother had saved enough money to send him to the best school in La Paz—San Calixto Jesuit High School. The Jesuits are a Roman Catholic order founded in Europe in the 1500s. In 1537, they came to Bolivia to set up missions and schools. Andres Santa Cruz, Bolivia's third president, donated the land and provided funds for the building of San Calixto School in the mid-1800s.

San Calixto was built on a hill near the presidential palace. The Jesuits not only taught practical subjects like mathematics and science, but also Christian virtues like social responsibility and charity.

Jaime's home was on a dry, run-down hillside. His home and the neighbors' dwellings were often in poor repair. When he began attending San Calixto, it was like entering a much different and more beautiful world. Plain walls surrounded the school, but inside were well-tended courtyards, refreshing water fountains, and even miniature fruit trees.

La Paz, Bolivia

La Paz is built in the shadow of towering snow-capped Mount Illimani. La Paz is the highest major metropolis in the world at an altitude of 12,001 feet (3,658 meters). By comparison, it is more than twice the altitude of America's highest large city, Denver, Colorado. The 1.5 million residents of La Paz live in a city where soaring skyscrapers and colorful outdoor shops coexist. Many Bolivians, especially young people, move to La Paz from the countryside seeking a better life.

The Bolivian city of La Paz sits at the foot of Mount Illimani.

San Calixto was very proud of the academic and athletic successes of its students. The walls were covered with ornamental plates calling attention to athletic championships and scholarly achievements. Although Jaime came from a family that struggled financially, he was bright and good at sports. It was not unrealistic for the ambitious boy to expect he, too, would find glory here.

For Jaime Escalante, Calixto was a wonderful, exciting experience. He was clever and intelligent, and he soon became a favorite of his teachers. In the all-male student body of 750 students, he quickly found a niche.

The wall around San Calixto was fifty feet high at the north end of the school patio. Jaime found it a perfect site for handball games during recess. When Jaime was scoring, he did not want the recess period to end, so he discovered a way to rig the school bell to ring later, after the game was over.

Jaime's love for boxing continued at San Calixto. His strong hands and powerful shoulders made him a tough competitor. He was always ready to take on a challenge from a fellow student. His reputation spread around the school, and when another boy would challenge him to prove how good he was, Jaime promptly took off his coat, handed it to a friend, and went into action. He almost always won the fight.

Jaime Escalante was popular at San Calixto, gathering around himself a group of loyal friends. The boys ate together and studied together. They were an

Jaime's family lived in the Sopocachi neighborhood of La Paz.

unofficial team with great spirit and enthusiasm. Having Jamie on the team was an asset to the other boys because of his intelligence and athletic prowess.

The taste for adventure and recklessness that led a younger Jaime Escalante to involve his little sister in those hair-raising escapades grew even stronger at San Calixto. Sara Escalante knew her son was very smart, but she feared his foolish side would be his undoing. Jaime seemed too fond of making jokes and laughing. But even when he became an adult, Jaime Escalante retained his wild sense of humor. In fact, he counted it as a great asset in his life. "Keep your sense of humor," he later told his own students. "Sometimes it will be your only link with sanity."[1]

It was not long before Jaime was passing his peers in class. He knew the material more quickly and more thoroughly than anyone else. The result was that he was getting bored as the teachers slowed down the lessons to help the less able students. Jaime wanted more advanced material, more challenging problems. His sister Olimpia was now studying chemistry and he borrowed her books. He was always eager to get to the next level in his studies.

At fifteen years old, Jaime discovered physics and loved it. He was in the fourth form year, which is the equivalent of tenth grade in American schools. A new teacher entered the boy's life and they bonded quickly. Father Descottes from France had a dry sense of humor that Jaime appreciated and a magical way of teaching.

He used electric motors, premeasured weights, and a small pendulum to enliven his classes. He did not just explain how science worked, he showed them. Jaime soon made a deal with his teacher. Father Descottes had brought from France wonderful old mathematics and science books that taught material far beyond Jaime's grade level. Jaime promised to keep the laboratory spotlessly clean if his teacher allowed him to borrow those books. Soon Jaime was leaping even faster ahead of the class as he devoured the material in the textbooks.

In spite of his love of learning in general and physics in particular, Jaime continued to be devoted to his pranks, which grew more dangerous as he was older. At a graduation celebration, he tossed a string of firecrackers under the gown of the school director. Jaime got into serious trouble for that mischief. If not for the frantic intervention of his mother's brother, Uncle Arturo, Jaime might have been expelled from San Calixto and forever derailed from his promising future.

The fact that Jaime was frequently in trouble in school made him sympathetic toward troublemaking students when he later met them as a teacher. As an adult, he confessed to preferring to teach students who had disciplinary problems because he could identify with them. "I understand those kids," he said. "I was suspended more than five times from junior high."[2]

One of Jaime's teachers at San Calixto was a boring lay teacher from Chile (most teachers at San Calixto were priests, but there were also a few laymen). He told long jokes in class, and on the next day, he would demand his students repeat the joke exactly as he had told it to prove they had been paying attention. Jaime could not resist repeating the jokes but adding considerably to them to the delight of his classmates. The teacher was not amused, however, and Jaime spent long periods standing out on the patio with his arms extended for punishment.

Many of the students at San Calixto were from wealthy backgrounds, and they did not socialize with those who were poorer. This did not prevent them from being friends with Jaime because he was so popular and capable that his humble beginnings never became an issue. He was accepted as one of the boys. But Jaime's classmates refused to ever socialize with the lower-class people who crowded the town square. There were shoeshine boys and beggars, and the upper-class San Calixto boys avoided them. Jaime, however, loved to mingle with all classes of people, especially the poor.

Even his mother did not approve of this. Sara Escalante, as a professional teacher, considered herself more respectable than lower-class Bolivians. She felt she had more status and that her family should cling to that as much as possible. She warned Jaime that if he made friends with the poor people in the square, this would undermine his own status later in life. Jaime's sisters gave him the same warning. Jaime ignored all this advice.

Eighteen-year-old Jaime Escalante, left, poses with his friend Victor on the San Calixto Jesuit High School grounds.

As a teenager, Jaime enjoyed going to the public square, which was teeming with colorful people selling food and trinkets. He loved to talk to the shoeshine boys and the merchants. He liked to ask them about their lives. He bought sodas and discussed sports and politics with the beggars, treating them no differently than he treated his friends at school. He believed there was something he could learn from even the poorest, most ragged stranger.

When a carpenter came to the Escalante house to do some repairs, Sara Escalante and her children kept their distance from the man. But Jaime made friends with him and watched him work. Jaime was fascinated by all the work the man could do, such as carpentry, electrical work, and plumbing. Later on, Jaime would use what he had learned from the man to build a little room for himself off the kitchen. It was adobe with a tin roof, but it gave the boy precious privacy for his studying.

Sara Escalante and her children attended early-morning Mass every Sunday, walking down the steep hill to church. After Mass, they trudged back up the hill and Sara Escalante made breakfast.

One time during breakfast, Sara Escalante placed some bread on the kitchen table and said to her children, "You divide this into four equal parts. One for Olimpia, one for Jaime, one for Bertha, one for Jose, one for me."[3] It saddened Jaime that his mother did not know how to divide the bread properly. It brought home

Escalante (in center, looking up) graduated from San Calixto Jesuit High School.

to him how even a teacher like his mother had been poorly trained in math.

Zenobio Escalante continued to visit his family. Despite his many shortcomings, he felt the need to keep some connection. Since he was usually drunk and in an angry mood, nobody looked forward to his visits. As a teenager, Jaime grieved that his father, an educated man, was sinking deeper into a sad and empty life.

One day, after coming to visit, Jaime's father collapsed on the couch of the family home at Sopocachi. Sara Escalante helped her husband from the couch to a bed. She told Jaime to go into town and get some medicine for his father. Neither Jaime nor his mother knew what was wrong with Zenobio, and because they did not call a doctor, it was never known. Because of his drinking and neglect of himself, his death the following day was no surprise.

The funeral took place a few days later. Jaime's sisters were weeping. Jaime looked at his mother in her black mourning dress. He thought about the hard life she had led raising her children alone. Jaime began to weep as well, but he knew he was not weeping for the loss of his father. He had lost him a long time ago. Jaime was weeping with relief that the strange, violent man his father had become would never again threaten the peace of the family.[4]

Teacher, Husband, Father

Nineteen-year-old Jaime Escalante was out of school and without work. He had dreamed of going to engineering school, but there was no hope of that. His widowed mother did not have the money to send him to college. The restless young man was suddenly caught up in something he had never planned. A revolution was going on in Bolivia and soldiers were being recruited. Escalante joined the army. He picked up his uniform and his weapons and headed for a battle he did not even understand. It was the government of Bolivia against the rebels who wanted more justice for the poor of Bolivia. Escalante was a government soldier during the few battles that were fought. Luckily, the rebellion ended quickly and the soldiers, including Escalante, were sent home. He still had no firm plans for his future.

Jaime Escalante was having lunch with an old friend, Roberto Cordero, when the subject of their futures came up. Cordero reminded Escalante how much he liked

In the photo at the top, Escalante (bottom right) sits with some fellow troops. In the bottom photo, Escalante (on right) and an army buddy pose with some friends.

Political Unrest in Bolivia

Ever since becoming a nation in 1825, Bolivia has been torn by wars and revolutions. The poverty of most of the people, especially the Indians, has contributed to the unrest. In 1951, Victor Paz Estenssoro tried to improve the working conditions of the poor in general and the country's miners in particular. He was overthrown and more revolutions followed. Recently there have been more bloody uprisings. A new president, Juan Evo Aima, has promised reforms to help all Bolivians.

physics, and he suggested Escalante look into teaching as a career. At first, Escalante rejected the idea, but then he recalled something his mother had said when he was a small boy. "If I give you money," she said, "you'll only spend it and it will be gone. If I teach you something—make you remember something—you'll have it forever."[1] Escalante began to see the profession in a new light. Escalante's mother was a teacher, and she took great pride in that. She felt it was important. Jaime Escalante decided to take the test for entrance to Normal Superior to study to become a teacher himself. Going to the school for teachers would cost money but not as much as engineering school. With the money he could earn at odd jobs and with some help from his family, Escalante thought he could manage it.

Escalante easily passed the entrance tests and began attending classes. The school was old and in poor repair. Everything was shabby and unreliable. The electricity often failed, plunging the classrooms into darkness when not enough sunlight could filter into the poorly ventilated rooms. Escalante often climbed onto the roof, cutting and splicing cables to get the lights back on. The classrooms were crowded with students as the children of poor families strove for the only chance they had of a professional career—teaching.

Jaime Escalante was in the second year at Normal when a physics instructor died at the American Institute, a school founded in 1907 by an American Methodist mission. It was a coeducational school, catering to both boys and girls, and it was operated like schools in the United States. Since Escalante was making excellent grades at Normal and seemed to show great promise, he was offered the job of replacing the physics teacher who had died.

Escalante leaped at the sudden opportunity. He would be making money to help with his school tuition at Normal. His mother was struggling to keep all her children in school and this would take some of the pressure off her. When Escalante visited the American Institute it reminded him of San Calixto. It had high walls and beautiful landscaping, something unusual in dry La Paz.

Jaime Escalante had never taught anything before when he walked into the classroom at the American

Institute. He was twenty-one years old, and he did not look any older than the students he would be teaching. It was a challenge. Escalante did not even know where the teacher who had died had left off in the course. Escalante did not know what he had covered or where to start. There was no textbook, and the dead teacher's notes were nowhere to be found. Escalante would have to teach the class using his old notes from San Calixto. The students would have nothing to study from but the lectures he gave and the notes they took.

On the first day, he faced the class at the American Institute, Jaime Escalante picked up a piece of chalk and began writing on the board. He was nervous and grim, but the students paid attention. Escalante soon learned, however, that although the students seemed attentive, they were not learning much. When he gave his first test, most of his students failed. Escalante set up after-school tutoring sessions for the students where he dealt with them individually. It was a practice that Escalante kept all through his teaching career. Soon the class was grasping the difficult material and doing much better on the tests.

Escalante and his friend Roberto Cordero spent much of their free time together hiking and attending parties. They hiked 328 miles to Copacabana four times, and then they hiked back again. The two young men were part of a group of friends from Normal School who enjoyed having a good time. Jaime Escalante, son of a man for whom drinking became a deadly demon, spent many evenings himself drinking with his friends. Escalante was twenty-two years old, yet he did not make the connection between his own use of liquor and what had become of his father.

The revolution that Jaime Escalante had briefly fought was again disrupting his life in Bolivia. Victor Paz Estenssoro's National Revolutionary Movement (MNR) was involved in three days of fighting, which spilled over into Jaime Escalante's neighborhood of Sopocachi. MNR rebels seized Sopocachi, and for a few days most people stayed off the streets. Large tracts of land were taken from companies and turned over to the Indians. The copper mines were nationalized. But, as the MNR was crushed, life continued as before.

Jaime Escalante was now a physics teacher at the National Bolivar School, a good public high school near the American Institute. At the National Bolivar School, Escalante developed the dynamic style of teaching with energetic lecturing interspersed with humor. He always knew what was going on in his classroom so things never got out of hand.

During this time, Jaime Escalante had a very busy social life. He enjoyed dating and was friendly with several young ladies. Escalante had a merry sense of humor and he always had a good time. When he finally became serious with one particular young woman, she was totally unlike his other girlfriends. Fabiola Tapia was a very quiet girl. She was the eldest daughter of a devoutly religious Evangelical Protestant family.

Escalante (left) always had an interest in sports. Besides teaching physics at National Bolivar School, he also coached the school's volleyball team.

Escalante was a Roman Catholic. The Tapia family did not want their daughter dating a Catholic.

Escalante and Tapia met when both were studying to be teachers. Her father was also a teacher and the author of many religious pamphlets on the Bible. No liquor was allowed in the Tapia household; however, Escalante had already developed a taste for wine with friends and family. Fabiola Tapia was a pretty, dark-haired girl, and in spite of her serious religious upbringing, something about Escalante's joyful personality appealed to her.

Soon Escalante and Tapia were dating in spite of their differences. He bought her *saltenas*—a favorite snack in Bolivia. It is made from thick yellow pastry dough held together by paper and wrapped around onion, beef, tomato, garlic, baby peas, beans, and eggs.

Escalante helped Tapia with her math homework and soon they were together all the time. He introduced her to his family. Olimpia and Bertha could not believe their fun-loving, prankster brother had chosen such a quiet and serious girl. Tapia's family was unhappy about Escalante's Catholic religion, but his gracious personality won their respect and they did not oppose the relationship.

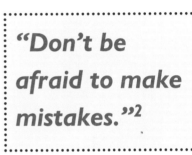

"Don't be afraid to make mistakes."[2]

In 1954, Jaime Escalante was offered a job teaching at San Calixto. He still did not have a teaching credential, but his reputation as an excellent teacher at the American Institute and the National Bolivar School was enough to recommend him. The twenty-three-year-old was fast becoming a legend in La Paz for his teaching skills. Also, he was fondly remembered as an outstanding student at San Calixto, and they were glad to see him coming back as a teacher.

Later, Jaime Escalante recalled his teaching days in La Paz, Bolivia, in the 1950s. "Early in my career I found that children learn better when learning is fun, when it is a game and a challenge," he said. "I cast the teacher in the role of a 'coach,'" Escalante said, calling

Escalante (on right) trained other physics teachers in Bolivia.

the students the team. When Escalante entered his students in academic competitions, he coached his team to defeat the opponent, which was the annual secondary school competition.[3]

When Jaime Escalante joined the faculty at San Calixto, he was also teaching afternoons at National Bolivar as well as later classes at Commercial High School. In addition, he tutored students and taught some evenings at a military academy. He never spared himself, and he expected his students to work hard, too. He told them he could not teach them without their help. He assigned between fifty and one hundred problems daily as homework, and he expected the work to be done.

Escalante bonded with his students as a coach does with his or her team. He played handball with them and encouraged them to share their personal problems. He tried to help resolve them. When students were not working to what he considered their potential, he would tell them, "You have entered San Calixto, but San Calixto has not entered you."[4] Jaime Escalante formed student teams for math, physics, and chemistry competitions, which provided strong motivation for the students.

On November 25, 1954, Fabiola Tapia and Jaime Escalante were married at the Calama Street Baptist Church in Cochabamba. Tapia walked down the aisle in a long white gown, and Escalante wore a black suit. The newly married Escalantes took a brief honeymoon and then moved into a small rented house close to Escalante's mother. The young couple did not have much money. In spite of all his teaching jobs, Escalante made a very modest salary, and his wife did not work. In 1955, Jaime, Jr., called Jaimito, was born.

Jaime Escalante had learned at an early age that a father owed his children love and nurturing. He was delighted at the birth of his son and eager to show the child the attention and encouragement he never received from his own father.

Jaime Escalante and Fabiola Tapia were married in 1954.

Fabiola Escalante loved her husband and new son, but she was concerned about her husband's social life. Jaime Escalante was a charming man with many friends and constant invitations to parties. While socializing with his friends, Escalante enjoyed drinking beer and playing cards. Neither of these activities pleased Fabiola Escalante, who had a strict Protestant upbringing. When the parents of Escalante's students invited him to a Christmas party, there were saltenas and beer for all. Escalante had a good time, but his wife was home worrying about it all. Fabiola Escalante did very little entertaining in the family home and there was never alcohol.

Fabiola Escalante's brothers had gone to southern California to study, and they sent back letters describing the good life there. She began to think her own husband should consider moving to the United States, too. She thought this move would separate Jaime Escalante from all his friends who were always inviting him to drinking parties. The family could live a quieter life in southern California. Fabiola Escalante thought it would be good for their son, too, because her brothers wrote of all the opportunities in the United States. The future for the Escalante family would not include beer parties. The political unrest that still existed in Bolivia would be behind them, too, and in the United States, wages would be much better for a man of Jaime Escalante's talents.

In 1961, the Escalantes moved to a new home in Sopocachi. It was a three-room duplex with a small kitchen that Jaime Escalante had built himself with his carpentry skills learned as a youth. The family also owned an old black DeSoto automobile. Jaime Escalante frequently took his small son on weekend trips at Lake Titicaca. There, father and son boated and ate shrimp from roadside stands. They mingled with the tourists and both had a good time. Jaime Escalante was very happy and leaving Bolivia did not seem like a good idea to him.

Jaime Escalante was enjoying teaching his classes. His students were winning important awards. He was always getting offers to do more tutoring. But Fabiola

Escalante often took his son on trips to Lake Titicaca in Bolivia.

Escalante had this dream of going to the United States. She was always talking about how much better it would be for the whole family if they left Bolivia. Escalante did not argue with his wife. He just listened and smiled and said nothing. But then Escalante was offered the chance to spend a year in Puerto Rico. He would be part of President John F. Kennedy's new program—the Alliance for Progress. It was a plan to improve conditions in South America. Under this program, improving education was seen as a way of fighting poverty. Bright young South American teachers like Escalante were needed to train the next generation of students.

Escalante enjoyed the experience of going to Puerto Rico. Until this time, he had never had the chance to travel outside his country. Now he studied in Puerto Rico. Then he traveled through eastern United States. He visited Niagara Falls and the White House, where he shook hands with President Kennedy. At this time, Kennedy was very popular in South America. He was young and vibrant. He seemed really interested in helping the people of South America.

When Jaime Escalante visited a high school in Tennessee, he was very impressed. The school had fine modern equipment in the science laboratories. Comparing this school to even the best schools in Bolivia saddened Escalante. He wished the young people of Bolivia and all of South America could attend such a school in their countries.

The year of studying in Puerto Rico and his travels through the United States changed Jaime Escalante. Before this he could not seriously imagine leaving Bolivia. But now he thought perhaps his wife was right. Her constant urging to move and settle in the United States began to make sense to Escalante.

The next time Fabiola Escalante talked about moving to the United States, her husband listened. He did not ignore her. When his wife spoke about how her brothers in southern California would help them get settled, Jaime Escalante made her a promise. If he could find a way to make the move, he would do it.

Jaime Escalante had his own reasons for being unhappy in Bolivia. Teachers received low wages. Although he worked at several jobs he could barely support his family. Revolutions were common.

Maybe, Escalante thought, it was time to go.

Coming to California

One particular incident can sometimes make a big difference. Just as Jaime Escalante was wavering about leaving Bolivia, something happened at San Calixto. Some of Escalante's senior students had taken a trip to Copacabana. The high-spirited boys had misbehaved. Escalante was disappointed and angry, but he did not want to see the boys expelled from San Calixto. He thought they were basically good young men. They did not deserve to have their futures damaged.

Jaime Escalante went to the administration at San Calixto and fought for his students. It was a tough fight. Escalante saved the boys from expulsion but bitterness remained on both sides. The administration resented Escalante for fighting so hard against the school's decision to punish the students. After so many harsh words, teaching at San Calixto was no longer the same. It was yet another reason to perhaps leave Bolivia and make a fresh start in the United States.

While Fabiola and Jaimito temporarily remained in Bolivia, Escalante moved to the United States. This is Jaime Escalante's photo from his passport.

Jaime Escalante met with his brothers, Felix and Raul, over dinner. It was time to talk with his family about the plans to move. "I have to leave this country," Jaime Escalante said with tears in his eyes. "Fabiola is right. My friends always call me up, have me out for a drink. I'm drinking too much."[1]

Finally Escalante had faced the fact that he was making some of the same mistakes his father had made. He had at last found the dangerous link between his drinking and partying and his father's tragic decline due to alcohol. The three Escalante brothers had always been close, and they understood what their brother was saying. However, they also felt sad that he would be going far away.

Fabiola Escalante hurried to pick up the necessary immigration papers. Only a certain number of immigrants from each country are legally admitted into the United States each year. The number is based on the population of the immigrant's country. Bolivia is a small country, so few immigrants are admitted. But in the year 1963, the Escalantes would be among them.

Samuel Tapia, Fabiola's younger brother, was already in southern California. He agreed to be the family's official sponsor. Someone who sponsors an immigrant must agree to help the newcomers financially so they do not become a burden to the country.

Jaime Escalante planned to go first. He would find a job and a place to live, then send for his family. Meanwhile, Fabiola and their son would live in Cochabamba with her family. Getting ready for the move, the

Escalantes sold all they had, including furniture. They owned a nice lot on which they planned to build a house, but that was sold, too. There was no turning back. They were going to make it in the United States.

The last day he spent in Bolivia was painful for Jaime Escalante. His sister Olimpia ironed his shirt so he would look nice when he arrived in the United States. The hardest part of all was leaving Sara Escalante, Jaime Escalante's mother. He could not bring himself to say good-bye to his mother in person. Sara Escalante knew her son would be leaving Bolivia, but she did not know just when. When the day came, Escalante wrote his mother a note. He wrote to *querida viejita* (my dear old lady). He told her she would always be in his mind and heart. Then he wrote: "God grant that I may return home someday." Sara Escalante kept that note under her pillow every night for the rest of her life.[2]

Jaime Escalante went to the airport and flew north on a Pan American DC-4. It was Christmas Eve, 1963, when he landed in Los Angeles. Sam Tapia picked him up at the airport and took him to his home in Pasadena.

Soon after arriving in Pasadena, Jaime Escalante noticed something he had never felt in Bolivia. The air was smoky and his eyes burned. Pasadena was one of the cities in southern California with heavy smog. Some days it was hard even to breathe the air.

Pasadena had something very helpful to new immigrants—Pasadena City College. The school opened in

Smog

Los Angeles and the small cities around it, like Pasadena, are built in a basin. Mountains surround the area. Polluted air gets trapped in the basin. In the 1950s, people living in southern California were allowed to have incinerators in their backyards. People could burn their paper and trash. This created little smokestacks coming from every yard. Also, old automobiles that are not well kept up give off more dangerous fumes than well-maintained cars. There was such heavy smog on some days that it was dangerous for children to play outside. Then laws were made to ban all the backyard incinerators. Smog checks had to be made on all cars to make sure they were in good working order. The air has improved because of this.

Members of Air Pollution Control measure the concentration of atmospheric pollutants in Los Angeles, California, on November 9, 1961.

1924 with less than five hundred students and fewer than a hundred teachers. It grew quickly, and by the 1950s, Pasadena City College was a fast-growing school. It offered classes to American and foreign-born students at low fees. Many newcomers, like Fabiola Escalante's brothers, learned English there. They also learned how to survive in their new country.

Escalante had three thousand dollars to start his new life. He spent twenty-four hundred of it on a pale green Volkswagen Beetle. Cars are necessary to get around in southern California. Escalante immediately began his job search. He could stay with Sam Tapia for now, but he needed a permanent home before he sent for his family.

Jaime Escalante was not having much luck in his job search before he finally got a job mopping floors at the Van de Kamp's restaurant in Pasadena. Sam Tapia had a hard time believing that this was the best his brother-in-law could do. Fabiola Escalante, Tapia's sister, had often told him how smart Jaime Escalante was. Surely there was something better for him than mopping floors. One of the major reasons why Escalante was having problems getting a good job was that he could not speak much English. Tapia insisted that Escalante come with him after work to Pasadena City College and enroll in night school.

Escalante asked for the mathematics entrance examination when he arrived at Pasadena City College. The instructor explained that it was a two-hour test. He told

Tapia to make it clear to his brother-in-law that he was not to ask any questions before the test was finished. He must work quietly on his own until the test was completed and ready to be handed in.

Jaime Escalante opened the test booklet and began working. The problems were easy for him. In less than thirty minutes, he was finished. He walked to the instructor's office and rapped on the door. He was scolded by the instructor who reminded him of the rules. It was a two-hour test and he was not to ask for help in the middle of it. The instructions had been very clear. Escalante, with the help of Tapia, explained that he had finished the test and now was handing it in. The instructor took the

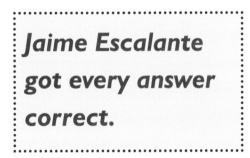

Jaime Escalante got every answer correct.

answer sheet and began correcting Escalante's test. He thought that someone who had turned in a two-hour test in thirty minutes had surely failed. But when he finished, the instructor looked at Escalante and delivered his verdict: Jaime Escalante got every answer correct.[3] He was now eligible to be admitted to Pasadena City College.

Jaime Escalante was now enrolled in college, he had a job, and Sam Tapia said he could live in his small guesthouse. It was time to send for Fabiola Escalante and their son. When they arrived, Escalante was too busy working to meet them at the airport. He had already been promoted at the Van de Kamp's restaurant,

Escalante enrolled at Pasadena City College.

and he was a cook. He was so important to the restaurant that they could not spare him even for a few hours. Escalante had made suggestions that had already improved business. He urged changes in the menu that would appeal to younger patrons. He noticed items on the menu that were not popular and should be dropped to raise profits. The boss was on the verge of making him manager.

Escalante was taking twelve units at Pasadena

City College, including English, mathematics, and electronics. He described those first days and weeks in class as "one of the most difficult semesters of my life." Adding, "After the classes were over, I always stayed either in the library or in the classroom until security asked me to leave. That was the only time I had for homework."[4]

When Fabiola Escalante first settled into the guesthouse her brother was providing, she was not completely satisfied. The bedroom was tiny and the kitchen and sitting room were too small. But what bothered her most was that her husband, an intelligent professional man, was working far beneath his talents. She was also bothered by the smog, which made her cough. Also, the people of Pasadena did not seem as warm and friendly as the people in Bolivia. But it was too late now for regrets. The family had to make it in the United States.

> "I picture life in this country as a cafeteria—you can pick anything you want, but you have to pay the price."[5]

Eight-year-old Jaimito Escalante liked southern California. But he also missed things about Bolivia, like the music. He played records of his favorite songs from home on the phonograph. Jaimito loved being with his father again. He enjoyed riding in the Volkswagen and sitting in the backseat as his mother learned to drive.

Jaimito was in fourth grade, but he knew no English. There was no one in the house who spoke English so there was no help there. Jaime Escalante later recalled that his son had to learn the language and he did. In "three years, the kid was swimming,"[6] Escalante boasted.

Jaime Escalante worked days at the Van de Kamp's restaurant and went to school at night. He recalled later, "I finished tired, but I knew that that was the right thing to do."[7] He was making a better salary at the restaurant than he had been making as a teacher in Bolivia. But his wife continued to be troubled. She felt it was not right that he should be doing the kind of work high-school students and uneducated men were doing.

Jaime Escalante wanted to return to teaching. That was the job he loved. He sent a letter to the California Department of Education listing all his teaching experience in Bolivia as well as his educational background. He had a valid teaching credential from Bolivia. The reply Escalante got was depressing. He was told that all his education in Bolivia meant nothing. His teaching experience and credential also meant nothing in the United States. If he wanted to teach in this new country, he would have to start all over again. He needed an American college education and a new teaching credential. Escalante would have to repeat his entire education—four years of college and a fifth year of graduate school for a

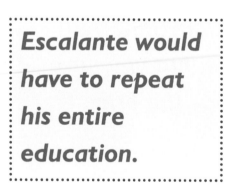

Escalante would have to repeat his entire education.

teaching credential. How could he do this and still work and support his family? Going to school part-time would probably take ten years, and Jaime Escalante was not young. He was in his mid-thirties. By the time he got his credential and was permitted to teach in the United States, he would be in his mid-forties.

Fabiola Escalante had one answer. She knew her husband had a dream of returning to teaching. This is what gave him his greatest fulfillment. But maybe this was not possible. He could find another way to use his brilliant mind. There was good money to be made in the electronics field.

Jaime Escalante considered his options. If the family returned to Bolivia, he could resume the work he loved—teaching. But now that Jaimito was adjusting so well to life in the United States it seemed a shame to pull him out of school. Surely future opportunities for the boy were much greater in the United States than in Bolivia. Fabiola did not find life in the United States entirely pleasing, but she did not want to return to Bolivia. That left the choice narrowed to two—continue at the restaurant and going to school or find a job in electronics and keep on trying to get that teaching credential. Jaime Escalante decided to investigate the electronics field.

Electronics and Education

Fabiola Escalante had gotten a job on the assembly line at Burroughs Corporation in 1967. Once called the Burroughs Adding Machine Company for its main product—adding machines—it was now one of the world's largest producers of computers. (Burroughs is now called Unisys Corporation.) The booming computer industry needed a lot of technicians. Jaime Escalante's wife told him he now spoke English better than many people at Burroughs who had good jobs. It was true that Escalante's English had improved greatly since attending Pasadena City College.

Fabiola Escalante related that computer parts often were breaking down on the assembly line. Somebody with electronics experience was needed. She thought her husband would be perfect for this job. Both Escalante's wife and son urged him to look for a job at Burroughs. Fabiola Escalante was still embarrassed to have her husband working at a restaurant.

Escalante was dong well in his college classes, and he kept reminding his wife, "This is all temporary."[1] But the dream of returning to the classroom seemed so distant. After spending two years at Pasadena City College, he was still a long way from an Associate of Arts degree. Then there would be two years at state college and a graduate school year. All this before he could return to teaching.

Jaime Escalante finally agreed to apply for a job at Burroughs. He was hired in the parts department. His job was to stock computer components and to deliver them to the foremen when needed. He was making less money than he made at the Van de Kamp's restaurant. At first, the job at Burroughs was very boring. Escalante soon found a way to make it more interesting. He reorganized the storage system, color coding all the parts. When somebody needed something they could locate it much more quickly.

One of the problems on the Burroughs assembly line was a failure of computer heads, where all the data was stored. There was a technician who dealt with those failures, but he was often absent. Escalante was given this job. He needed some time to learn all the details, but once he grasped it he was very efficient. He was soon promoted to senior tester of equipment. The suggestions Escalante made to streamline procedures and cut costs were excellent. Escalante was always moving up and down the work stations in his long white coat and cap. In everything he did, Jaime Escalante tried to do it

Escalante worked hard to earn his Bachelor of Arts degree in mathematics from California State University. Above are a bookstore and food court on the campus.

better than it had been done before. He was proud of his work. He was pursuing excellence all the time. He said later, "Never stop testing your talents, never be afraid to test your limits. Successful people go beyond their own limits."[2]

In 1969, Escalante graduated from Pasadena City College with his associate's degree. After many years of teaching, Escalante said that the degree from Pasadena

City College in engineering is the document he prizes above all others, even the awards he has received.[3]

In 1969, the Escalantes welcomed their second son, Fernando. Fourteen-year-old Jaimito was becoming interested in electronics and he often discussed engineering problems with his father. Eventually, Jaimito would also attend Pasadena City College.

By 1972, Escalante was so well respected at Burroughs that he was offered the supervisor's job at a new plant the corporation was opening in Guadalajara, Mexico. At the time, Escalante was about a year away from receiving his Bachelor of Arts degree from California State University. He turned down the job offer.

Escalante had enjoyed working at Burroughs. He liked the challenge of doing new things. But after all these years, the work had gotten boring. Escalante was working with equipment and computer papers. What he longed to do was work with people, with students whom he could motivate to do great things. In 1973, Escalante graduated from Cal State with a degree in mathematics. His dream of returning to teaching was coming within his grasp. But he was not there yet.

One of Escalante's professors at Cal State told him he had the talent to go as far as he wanted to go in the electronics field. Escalante said he would rather teach. His professor then called his attention to an excellent opportunity: The National Science Foundation Scholarship.

National Science Foundation
The National Science Foundation (NSF) was created by Congress in 1950 as an independent federal agency. The goals were "to promote the progress of science; to advance the national health, prosperity, and welfare; to secure the national defense."[4] In many areas like mathematics, computer science, and the social sciences, NSF is the primary source of federal backing. The NSF has the task of keeping the United States on the leading edge of discovery in everything from astronomy to zoology.

The scholarship was offered to gifted people seeking to teach. It would allow the recipient to study full-time at a university and college. If Jaime Escalante won this scholarship, it meant he could be teaching within a year.

Fabiola Escalante was not very supportive of her husband's idea of quitting Burroughs and going full-time for his teaching credential. She was not so sure that winning the scholarship would be a good thing. Jaimito brought home many stories of wild, unruly students in his classes. Many teachers could not keep the classrooms quiet enough for any real learning to take place. She thought American teenagers were not as respectful of their teachers as the youth in Bolivia were. Fabiola Escalante worried that her forty-two-year-old husband could not handle these rowdy students. He would be a failure at teaching, and then what would happen?

Jaime Escalante went for the scholarship anyway. He later said he loved teaching because "[t]eaching is touching life."[5] Even though Escalante would be making less money if he was hired as a teacher than he was making at Burroughs, his wife knew he had to do what was right for him. Fabiola Escalante long argued for the family to leave Bolivia and come to the United States. She won that argument. But she would not fight for this. She had talked her husband into going into the electronics industry, but if his heart was elsewhere, she would support him.

Jaime Escalante had to pass a three-part examination as he competed for the scholarship. The mathematics and physics examinations were the easiest. He never had any problem proving himself in those areas. The

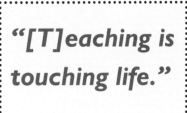

"[T]eaching is touching life."

second part of the test was oral—Escalante had to explain his philosophy of education. Once again this was no problem. He had a strong philosophy and he passionately believed in it. "A teacher must possess love to be able to accomplish. The students see my passion to the subject and my passion to teach,"[6] he said. He described three things a teacher must have. "Number one is the knowledge of the subject. The second thing is I have to motivate. Third, you have to understand human relations."[7]

The third and final part of the test was the most

challenging. It was a demonstration of teaching skills observed by the committee who chose the scholarship winner. Fifteen college students were chosen to play the roles of bored and unruly teenage high-school students. Escalante and four other finalists were asked to prepare a thirty-minute mathematics lesson. They had to present it to the class while dealing with the discipline problems. The level of discipline they were able to achieve had to be sufficient to get the lesson across.

When Escalante entered the mock classroom, two students were scuffling in one corner of the room. Escalante approached the students holding out his arms as if he was about to hug them. He did not scold the students. Instead he said it was wonderful that they were fighting to prove their manhood. He said he had been quite a fighter in his own youth. Escalante cheerfully told the students to return to their desks. As soon as class was over, he promised, he would take them both outside and fight each of them in turn. The students returned to their desks.

Jaime Escalante then introduced himself. He now spoke good English, but with a heavy accent. The scholarship committee watched intently as he began his lesson.

Escalante launched into a discussion of shortcuts the students could take so they would not need to memorize the times tables. The students were attentive. Escalante looked straight at each student as his gaze

Escalante decided to teach at Garfield High School because it was in an area where a lot of Latino students lived.

roamed around the room. His lively tone of voice and mischievous grin seemed to captivate the students.

During the lesson, when restlessness broke out in the classroom, Escalante switched to math tricks. Again he grabbed the attention of his students. He concluded the class with a discussion of subtraction. Students were asking questions and participating.

Jaime Escalante won the scholarship. He spent the following year in teacher preparation classes. In 1974, he finally had in his hands the document he had struggled for eleven years to get, a California teaching credential. Now at last, the forty-three-year-old Escalante would return to the career he loved.

Jaime Escalante needed to find a job. He headed for an interview with the Los Angeles Unified School District that would put him back in the classroom. As soon as introductions were done, the interviewer showed Escalante a map of the Los Angeles school system. He pointed out where various ethnic groups were concentrated. Escalante was interested in teaching in a Latino school.

Escalante was offered a position in three schools, each having a large Mexican-American enrollment: Belvedere Junior High, Roosevelt Senior High, and Garfield Senior High.

Escalante chose Garfield Senior High School.

Garfield High School

When Jaime Escalante visited Garfield High School for the first time, he admired the jacaranda trees dropping their lavender blooms onto the lawns. He also liked his new principal—Alex Avilez. He seemed like someone Escalante could really work with. To Escalante's pleasure, he was hired as a computer teacher. This is just what he wanted. He understood computers and he was excited about them. He wanted to pass on that excitement to students who were heading into a computer-dominated world. Everything seemed to be going right for Escalante.

But in September 1974, when Escalante reported for work and saw his schedule of classes for the first time, he was surprised. He learned he would be teaching five periods of basic math. Escalante mentioned the fact that he had been hired to teach computers. He was told the computer program was on hold. He would just have to teach basic math. Escalante's disappointments were only beginning. He was sent to a conference room

Garfield High School

Garfield High School was built in 1925 in East Los Angeles when the area was quite rural. Over the years, the population of Los Angeles County grew. The great majority of the student body was Mexican American. Many of the families were recent immigrants to the United States. Some of them were there illegally. Although the neighborhood around Garfield featured tree-lined streets and pastel stucco homes, there was widespread poverty. There was also serious trouble with gangs. Graffiti defaced many walls and store buildings.

John Ortiz, a Mexican-American student leader at Garfield High School, addresses students during a walkout protest on March 7, 1968.

where he met his fellow math teachers. They were discussing new methods for teaching math. Escalante listened in disbelief. The teachers were saying the students would be asked to cut out and measure pictures of familiar household objects. After that they would do puzzles. Escalante watched the other math teachers busily putting the puzzles together. He thought he was back in primary school in Bolivia.

As Escalante made his way to his classroom, he wondered if this is what it would be like teaching in the United States. He thought perhaps he had made a mistake after all leaving the Burroughs Corporation. And then he met his class.

Escalante was shocked by his students. He recalled later, "They were using their fingers adding stuff on the board. They came in without supplies, with nothing. Total chaos."[1] Some of the students were chatting loudly and totally ignoring the teacher who had just entered the room. Others were fighting, using some of the foulest language Escalante had ever heard. The students were behaving as if this was a normal part of their school routine.

Escalante began going around the room addressing individual students. In a strong but friendly voice, he demanded to know what they wanted to accomplish in life. He joked with them about some of his own school pranks. As Escalante looked around the room he noticed ugly graffiti everywhere. The room was messy and disorganized. Escalante started talking about one of his own passions, the Los Angeles Lakers basketball team. He suggested to the students that colorful posters of Lakers stars would be good around the room. Most of the students liked the Lakers, too. Escalante bonded with them over this common interest. Then Escalante said the room would need to be cleaned up before he brought in his posters. Graffiti needed to be scraped from desks and walls. The room needed cleaning and painting. Escalante grinned at the students and asked which of them would come on Saturday to help him put this classroom in shape. Hands shot up all around him. By the following Saturday, the learning environment was changed. But this was only the beginning.

Most of the students in Escalante's class were totally bored. They did not like learning. They did not dream much about the future. When Escalante asked them what they wanted to be in life, they stared at him. "Where is the money?" Escalante growled, though his eyes danced. Again they had no answer. Escalante provided the answer. "The money is in chemistry, physics, computers, electronics." Then Escalante said he would make a deal with the students. He would teach them math and "with that you're going to make it."[2]

Ordinary teaching methods would not reach these students. However, Escalante was not an ordinary teacher. When his class seemed bored he whipped out an apron and a chef's hat (which he kept from his days at the Van de Kamp's restaurant) and wielded a large butcher's knife. He placed an apple on his desk and chopped it into sections. "Let's talk about percentages," he said, and the students, amazed by the sight of their teacher in a chef's costume, were on his side.[3]

Sometimes Escalante put on music to get the class in the mood for learning. He often used the song "We Will Rock You." The students kept time with the song, pounding on their desks. Then Escalante swung into his lesson. He was always using something students could relate to so that he could get their attention. He motivated them by "something the kids like to do," he said.[4] Escalante compared math concepts with some sports terms. The three-point shot was like a parabola (a curve

> **"Look, your future is not to become Michael Jordan. Your future is to become a superstar engineer or technician."[5]**

formed by cutting a cone with a plane parallel to one of its sides). The three-second violation in basketball was absolute value in math. A face-mask penalty, as in football, meant you made a mistake when you began a problem.

Jaime Escalante's unusual methods extended to the use of a little red pillow that he hurled at students who appeared inattentive during class. A tardy student often found himself sitting in a kindergartner's desk, which Escalante kept in the room for this purpose. Once they

Because Escalante wears it so much, the type of hat he is wearing in this photo is now called an "Escalante hat" in Bolivia.

had to sit in the little chair, Escalante noted, "they don't come to class late anymore."[6]

Escalante used many of the same techniques he had used at San Calixto to motivate his students. He was especially determined to reach students others thought were "unteachable." Escalante picked fights with the students over their hair or their choice of clothing. This aroused a student's anger and then his curiosity. Why is this teacher bothering with me, the student would wonder. Most teachers simply ignored the students who seemed beyond help. Most teachers spent their energy on the students who seemed to be cooperating. Escalante seemed to genuinely care about them. This passion lifted them from their apathy or despair.

Escalante played handball with his students after classes. He told them that if he won they would have to do their homework. If they won they would get an automatic A. It did not seem possible to the students that Escalante would win, but he always did. He was an excellent athlete. Every Saturday morning at nearby Griffith Junior High handball court, contests would be held. The middle-aged teacher never had to hand out an automatic A. All this effort and attention that Escalante put into his students convinced them that he really did care about them. Years later, Sergio Valdez of Escalante's class of 1991 said, "Mr. Escalante even let me bring my sister into summer classes when I had to baby-sit. And that was okay with him. He lived for his students, and he was determined to see them succeed."[7] (Valdez became an engineer employed by NASA's Jet Propulsion Laboratory in Pasadena.)

The administration at Garfield often did not know quite how to handle Escalante. He created a system where a student would have to answer a homework question before he was admitted to class. When the administration found out about this, they confronted Escalante. He explained, "I have to find ways to make them learn." The administration retorted, "Just get them inside!" Escalante shot back, "There is no teaching, no learning going on here. We are just baby-sitting."[8]

In 1974, conditions at Garfield were terrible. Gangs had divided the school into zones where they ruled. They planned attacks on one another within the school. Hundreds of Garfield students dropped out before graduation, facing a bleak future. When Jaime Escalante asked for better textbooks, he was politely turned down. He was told the students at Garfield could not handle harder material. They would just be frustrated.

In the summer of 1975, Escalante worked at two electronics plants. Sometimes it seemed that he had already burned out from teaching at Garfield and would return permanently to the electronics field. But in Escalante's heart he knew this would not happen. He would return to Garfield and try even harder the next school year.

On the first day back at Garfield, Escalante put up new posters and tried new techniques. The principal had been transferred and the new principal was Paul Possemato. If Possemato could not turn Garfield from its downward spiral, the school was in danger of losing its accreditation. Teams of educators regularly study schools every few years to make sure they are providing an adequate education. If a school is shown to be very

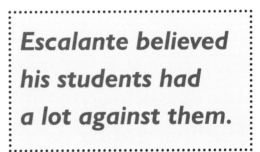

Escalante believed his students had a lot against them.

inadequate and not providing a good education it loses its accreditation. This is a serious blow to every graduate of that school. Their diplomas are not taken as seriously as are diplomas from schools with accreditation.

Possemato cleaned up the school graffiti and made sure gang symbols were no longer scrawled on the walls. He kept nonstudents off the campus. Doors and entrances were locked. Possemato had heard good things about Escalante. He liked what Escalante had done in his classroom. Escalante wanted to help the new principal succeed. Escalante and other teachers gladly patrolled the school halls to keep students in their classrooms and stop fights.

Escalante believed his students had a lot against them before they even came to school. They were poor, uneducated, and many of them lived in fear of immigration officers, because they were not legal residents of the country. On top of all that, Escalante worried that the students were looking for an easy way to get by in life and were not willing to work hard. "They look for a job to buy a car and that's it. Nothing else," he lamented.[9]

A new teacher, Henry Gradillas, became dean of discipline at Garfield. He worked well with Escalante to improve the environment at school. One day, a young

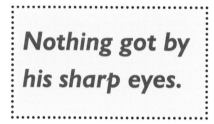

Nothing got by his sharp eyes.

mathematics teacher, Ben Jimenez, was desperately trying to teach, but his class was in an uproar. He could not be heard over the students. Jimenez visited Escalante's classroom and was impressed by the quiet. Escalante offered to trade classes with Jimenez for a few days. Escalante marched into Jimenez's classroom and down the rows of desks. He ripped magazines from the hands of startled students. He yelled at them. When Jimenez reclaimed his class, he found his students humbled. Jimenez and Escalante were partners working together to improve discipline at Garfield.

The key to Escalante's success was quick, tough action the moment a problem broke out. He kept the students busy, and he was always on top of the situation. Nothing got by his sharp eyes. Escalante also understood the students and knew all about their neighborhoods. He knew the names of their gangs and where they were located. He even found out the gang nicknames of some students. He liked to shock a gang member by calling on him in class by his gang name. And then Escalante did simple things, too, like passing out candy in class as a reward for a good day.

In the summer of 1976, Jaime Escalante took Fabiola and their two boys back to Bolivia to visit their families. Sara Escalante was in the hospital with heart problems, but the doctors were optimistic about her recovery. Jaime Escalante had not been back to the country in twelve years and the family was overjoyed to see him. Jaimito was a twenty-one-year-old college student. Fernando was seven years old. Escalante was forty-six, and his sisters were surprised by how he looked. They had said good-bye to their youthful brother more than a decade ago. Now they found him looking middle-aged. He was heavier than he had been and he was balding.

The vacation in Bolivia was delightful. There were many reunions and parties. It was like the good old days for Jaime Escalante with folk music and saltenas. Escalante went to Lake Titicaca, introducing his younger son to the beautiful lake where he and Jaimito spent many wonderful weekends years before. Jaimito remembered quite a bit about Bolivia, but it was all new to Fernando.

When it finally came time for the Escalantes to leave, tears of sadness flowed. It was especially hard on Jaime Escalante's sister, Bertha. She did not want to part from the brother with whom she had shared so many child-hood adventures.

Jaime Escalante returned to Garfield High School for his third year. With tighter discipline and an improved curriculum, the school had been spared the loss of accreditation. Escalante was ready to do even greater things. He had already achieved good results, but he was shooting for excellence. To his students, he defined excellence as "Do the right thing the first time. You take the test the first time. Bang! You stand and deliver."[10]

The Advanced Placement Class

In 1955, the first Advanced Placement (AP) classes were offered in the United States. At first, most were available only at private schools on the East Coast. The idea was to allow bright high school students to take college-level classes. By completing these advanced classes and passing a test to prove they had gained the knowledge, the students received college credits while still in high school. This helped them skip introductory classes in college. It was seen as a way to challenge high school students to excel.

In his second year at Garfield High School, Jaime Escalante learned of the Advanced Placement program. There had been a few halfhearted efforts to offer an Advanced Placement math class at Garfield, but most of the teachers did not believe the students could master such a class. Escalante was asked if he would be interested in teaching an Advanced Placement calculus class. He was not immediately enthusiastic. He knew that the students at Garfield were not receiving the kind of math that would prepare them for such a demanding course. But the idea slowly grew appealing to Escalante. He was always looking for ways to motivate his students. And competitions in Bolivia had inspired his San Calixto students to rise to new levels.

Jaime Escalante finally decided he liked the idea. An AP calculus test would be a good thing. "Because it tells us that we teachers are doing the job," he said. "I could tell you I'm the best teacher because all my kids got As. The test is important to prove I'm doing that."[1]

Advanced Placement Classes

More than fifty percent of America's twenty-four thousand high schools offered Advanced Placement classes in 2006. The courses were in thirty-seven subjects from English to math. Enrolled students take standardized tests in the spring to decide if they had learned enough in their courses to earn college credits.

Although Latino students are taking Advanced Placement tests at about the same rate as their percentage of the student body, they are not passing the AP tests at a high rate. Experts say that because Latinos are not receiving good basic education in the lower grades, they are not prepared for the tough AP tests.[2]

Escalante began preparing for the AP class, but before he even started, he hit a roadblock. He had to get better textbooks for his students. Otherwise they would have no chance of mastering the tough material in the class. Escalante was using a book called *Consumer World*. It was a pleasant book and helpful in introducing students to basic math concepts, but it could not be used to train AP students. Escalante pleaded for a more advanced textbook, but the administration refused. When the current principal was transferred, Garfield got a new principal who seemed to like Escalante. She sent him a letter praising his teaching skills. Still no adequate textbook was offered, however.

Escalante took the glowing letter she sent him to her office. He told her he had no use for only her praise. Would she please replace her kind words with new textbooks for his students? It would cost three thousand dollars to buy the books Escalante needed. The principal told him the school did not have the money. Escalante then said he wanted to transfer to another school. He could no longer teach at a school where they refused to meet the needs of their students. The principal then promised to see what she could do. She contacted a parents' group and the teachers' union.

> *"Calculus need not be made easy. It is easy already,"*
> —*a poster in Escalante's classroom.*[3]

Together they raised the money. Escalante got the new textbooks for his AP class. Now he could lift his students to a higher level where they had a chance to succeed.

Jaime Escalante recruited his first AP class in the fall of 1978. He was enthusiastic as he tried to convince his math students to enter the AP calculus class. Escalante gathered fourteen students for his first class.

However, when he got a copy of the test these students would have to pass next spring, he was crushed. He knew they could never pass such a test without incredible effort. He had eight months to get them in shape. He wondered if they could commit themselves to what he would demand. He called the fourteen students together and told them they did not know nearly enough. They would have to study harder than they had ever studied before. Then, Escalante outlined the tough study schedule ahead. He would begin teaching every day thirty minutes before the regular school day began. There would be a five-minute quiz every day. A test would be given every Friday.

Seven of the fourteen students dropped the course over the next two weeks. It was just too much for them. Then two more left. Jaime Escalante now had three girls and two boys in his class. He coaxed them along, encouraging them. He used all the gifts he had as a teacher. He bullied them and praised them. He appealed to their pride. Did they want to be the first successful AP calculus class ever at Garfield High?

What an honor this would be. Later, one of Escalante's math students, Maria Torres, recalled the magic of his methods. "Many teachers merely instruct you," she said, "Mr. Escalante's secret is he really cares. He made us feel powerful, that we could do anything."[4]

Escalante cultivated his small class like a gardener protects precious flowers. He put them through the paces until at last it was the spring of 1979. The five pioneers trooped into the test room on that May morning. After the AP calculus exam was done, the students came out of the room looking stunned. They had been through a harrowing experience. They knew it would be hard but they did not think it would be this tough.

Escalante teaches a class at Garfield High School on August 10, 1983.

Escalante waited for the results of his daring experiment. The five students had deep doubts that they had passed the test. The Educational Testing Service (ETS) in Princeton, New Jersey, used a scale of 1 to 5 in their grading system. A score of 3 or better was needed to pass and get college credit. In Escalante's first class, there were two 4s and two 2s. There was one 1. That meant two of his students would get college credit. They had proved it could be done. They had shown that students with poor backgrounds in math could work hard enough to pass this most difficult test. "My students rose to the level of my expectations," Escalante said many times. "If we expect winners, they become winners. And if we expect losers, they act like losers. Our expectations can give our kids roots and wings."[5]

But Jaime Escalante was determined to do even better next time. This was only the beginning. Escalante's friend and colleague, Ben Jimenez, was more confident in the classroom. He was doing well preparing the groundwork for the next AP calculus class. In the fall of 1979, Escalante assembled a group of nine students. He worked even harder than before to get them ready for the May 1980 exam. Six of the nine passed with college credit. The May 1981 results were more promising yet. Fifteen students took the AP calculus test and fourteen passed with college credit. Another landmark happened when one of Escalante's students got a perfect 5. It was Raquel Soto, who later became Escalante's assistant.

Jaime Escalante was now on fire with excitement. The math concepts he was teaching were very difficult, and he looked for ways to make them more appealing. He wanted the classes to have an element of fun to ease the pressure on the students.

Escalante fashioned a two-dimensional cardboard cutout of Charlie Brown, the hero of the beloved *Peanuts* comic strip. The figure had moving jaws that made it appear to be speaking. Escalante got some of the tough math concepts across to his students through the cardboard lips of his Charlie Brown puppet. The students understood what he was trying to do—lighten the high-pressure atmosphere. The better students may have thought this strategy silly. But even they understood what their teacher was trying to do. And the good students admitted that hearing it from Charlie Brown may have made it a little easier to remember.

Escalante alternated his tactics. Along with threatening his students that if they failed they faced a lifetime of working in a fast-food restaurant, he also used humor and gentle persuasion. He ran his classes rigidly. One of the things Escalante loved most about mathematics was its orderliness. He started each class with a five-minute quiz. All of the Garfield students joining the AP calculus team had to sign a paper listing promises. They had to be attentive, do their homework, and do their very best. Escalante also involved the parents. They all knew their children were part of an important project. Escalante once said about bringing parents into the job of

Jaime Escalante gives students advice in one of his classes.

education, "That kid belongs to you. He doesn't belong to the state or the school; he's your kid. So you have to help me out to raise this kid."[6]

When Escalante announced the tough schedule to the AP calculus team, some students tried to get out of the class. Escalante had a new strategy. He told them they could not get out. According to school policy they did have a right to pull out. However, Escalante enlisted the aid of sympathetic counselors to back him up on his "no escape" clause.

Escalante was a strong man in generally good health, though he suffered from occasional gallbladder attacks. He had been diagnosed with gallstones—

stonelike formations in the gallbladder—a pear-shaped organ near the liver. (Gallstones sometimes cause liver trouble or severe pain. They are usually removed through surgery.) Escalante was always so busy with his students that he ignored the brief episodes and continued to push himself.

Jaime Escalante could be tough and frightening to students, or he could sweet talk them into cooperation. Daniel Schugurensky researched Escalante's methods for his Department of Adult Education. He said Escalante was "a demanding teacher, a counselor, or a friend, depending on the student and the circumstance."[7] Schugurensky related that when a student was overwhelmed, Escalante would say to him, "You are the best, you are the hope for the future. Remember that."[8]

> "You are the hope for the future."

Jaime Escalante had many confrontations with the school administration. After one particularly bad one, he said he was going to apply to another school and transfer there. He loved the AP calculus program and he thought he might have more progress with it in another school. Escalante applied to Monrovia High School, but he was not offered a job. He then rolled up his sleeves and worked even harder at Garfield. He would somehow make his dream of a larger AP calculus class at Garfield come true.

A Crisis in the AP Class

In 1981, Jaime Escalante was elected by his fellow teachers to be chairman of Garfield High School's math department. The job included many details and meetings. For busy teachers like Escalante, the honor was overshadowed by the work. Escalante was never one to busy himself with paperwork. He preferred using all his time and energy for hands-on teaching. He told his colleagues from the start that he would take the job but skip many of the meetings. He considered them a waste of time.

Escalante was in the process of preparing his largest AP calculus class yet—with eighteen students who would take the May 1982 exam. There were ten boys and eight girls. Most of the AP calculus class was at least part Mexican. When a testing fee of twenty-one dollars was suddenly added, Escalante knew many of his students could not afford it. For some, it would mean dropping out of class. Escalante held candied apple sales and car washes so nobody had to drop out for economic reasons.

Then Escalante began the hard work of coaching his new team.

One of the juniors, Leticia Rodriguez, was an excellent math student, but she was on the edge of quitting the AP class because of a heavy work schedule. There were seven children in her family. Leticia worked several shifts at the restaurant her parents ran in downtown Los Angeles. Leticia not only had little time for homework, but in the crowded family home she had nowhere to study. All this left her exhausted and struggling to cope with the tough study schedule that Escalante demanded. Escalante did not want to lose any member of the team, but especially not Leticia. She was bright and likely to do well in the AP test. Escalante saw a good future for her. However, Leticia's parents were urging her to drop out of the AP class. They needed her at the restaurant because she was a good worker and trustworthy.

One night, Jaime Escalante and Ben Jimenez went to the Rodriguez restaurant to talk to Leticia's parents. First they spoke with her mother. Escalante explained that this young woman could become an engineer, a physicist, or a teacher, but she needed more time to study. Leticia's father then joined in the conversation. He said that women did not need an education as men did. Women got married and their husbands took care of them. Escalante pleaded with Leticia's parents not to shut the door on her bright future. Leticia's father walked away.

Escalante and Jimenez were sad when they left the restaurant. They were sure the parents had not accepted their pleas and Leticia would be forced from the calculus team. She would lose her big chance for a good career. The next morning, however, Leticia Rodriguez came to class smiling. Her parents reduced her work schedule at the restaurant. They even planned to buy her a desk so she could study better. Leticia could remain on the AP calculus team.

Henry Gradillas was the new principal at Garfield High School, and he was very helpful in getting Escalante the materials he needed to train his students. Gradillas also improved the whole math program at Garfield. There were more advanced math classes and less basic math.

As Escalante drilled his team, it was a stressful time for him. In March 1982, Jaimito Escalante heard his father going back and forth to the kitchen all night. Something was wrong. Twenty-six-year-old Jaimito, now an engineer at Teledyne, still lived with the family. When his father appeared in the morning for breakfast, he looked pale. Jaimito urged him to call the school and say he was too sick to come in.

Jaime Escalante refused to skip school, especially at this crucial time. The May AP tests were just two months away. Every day counted. Escalante had too much to do during the next weeks. Anyway, Escalante had felt like this before. He toughed his way through the pain and went on working.

By midday, Escalante was in more pain than he had ever felt before. His left side hurt so much he had to sit down. When he tried to stand up again, the pain worsened. Escalante assigned problems from the textbook for the remainder of the day. After the students left the classroom, Escalante slumped over his desk in terrible pain. When the AP calculus team came for their afternoon drill at 2:00 P.M. Escalante remained at his desk as they worked on problems from the board. At 6:00 P.M., he met his night-school class, but the pain in his left side was now unbearable. He left the classroom to go to the drinking fountain on the next floor. As he walked down the steps, Escalante became dizzy, losing his grip on the handrail. He slipped and stumbled down the rest of the way, hitting the floor below. For a few minutes, Escalante was unconscious.

The night-school students did not know what was happening. They worked at their seats waiting for their teacher to return. Escalante finally regained consciousness. He stood up and made it to the water fountain, splashing water on his bloody face. He cleaned the blood from the cut over his eye. He mopped up the blood on the floor with tissues.

With difficulty, Escalante made it to Ben Jimenez's classroom. He asked his friend to keep an eye on the night-school class and to tell the principal that Escalante had gone home sick. Escalante reminded Jimenez to lock the classroom when the period ended.

Jimenez pleaded with Escalante to let him take him home. Escalante refused. He got in his Volkswagen and, fighting the pain all the way, made it safely home. But he was hurting so much he could not get out of the car for several minutes. Finally he gained the strength to drag himself inside.

Escalante had put off the surgery to have his gallstones removed and now he was suffering the worst attack ever. Jaimito Escalante drove his father to the hospital emergency room. Escalante spent the night at the hospital. The doctor told him that he had suffered a heart attack. Escalante laughed at the diagnosis and demanded to leave the hospital so he could get back to work. The doctors insisted he needed more bed rest, but Escalante called his wife to come pick him up. Fabiola Escalante drove to the hospital expecting to take her husband home to recuperate. Instead he slid into the driver's seat, drove her home, and rushed down to Garfield High.

Word had spread among the AP calculus class that Jaime Escalante had fallen down the stairs after suffering a heart attack. When he marched into the classroom wearing a big bandage over his eye, his students were amazed to see him. They believed he had shrugged off a heart attack to rejoin them. The incident increased the awe many of the students felt for Escalante. He seemed like a super human. In fact, some of the students called him Kimo, short for Kimo Sabe, which was another spelling for Kemo Sabe, the name the Lone

Ranger's partner, Tonto, called him. The Lone Ranger was a cowboy hero in the comics and the movies.[1]

Escalante did nothing to correct the confusion about his medical problem. He decided to use it to further motivate the class. "You see! You see!" he chanted, "You burros [donkeys] gave me a heart attack. But I come back. I'm still the champ."[2]

All of the AP calculus students eventually accepted Escalante's work ethic. They came to school at 7:00 A.M., attending math drill and then class. At 2:50 P.M., when the rest of the school went home, they stayed until 5:00 P.M. for more intensive study. Escalante talked about the May test as the big game. He drilled his students and joked with them. He was not only a teacher, but a coach, a big brother, an uncle, even a father.

Tension grew as the test neared. As they prepared for the AP calculus test, most of the students were also making plans about what college they planned to attend. Some had already been offered scholarships. If a female student was offered a scholarship that would take her far from home, her protective Latino family would not permit her to accept it.

The night before the test, Jaime Escalante told everyone to have a good meal and a good night's sleep. That was easier said than done for the nervous students and for Escalante as well.

The students marched into Room 411 for the big test in the morning. Most of them felt confident after they had taken the test. They believed they had done

Escalante's entire 1982 AP calculus class passed the Advanced Placement calculus exam.

well. All that drilling paid off. They were very well prepared.

The proctor who oversaw the test gathered up the eighteen calculus exams. They were placed in a special AP mailing envelope and sent to the Educational Testing Service in Princeton, New Jersey, for grading.

Escalante and the eighteen students waited anxiously for the results. Would anybody earn a 5? How many would earn 4s? Would they all pass? Would this be Jaime Escalante's greatest triumph, bringing all eighteen students through to success?

Within a week, the result letters began arriving at the homes of the AP students. Seven students, including

Leticia Rodriguez, received a 5. But in the midst of their happy celebrations, another letter arrived. This second letter threatened to destroy everything they had worked for. The Educational Testing Service now doubted the validity of some of the tests. They had indications that students had copied from one another. They believed that cheating had taken place.

Jaime Escalante was with his family on Orange Avenue in Monrovia when he got the terrible news. The phone rang and Escalante listened in disbelief as a hysterical student told him about the letter accusing the student of cheating. Escalante asked if anybody had cheated. The student denied it had happened. Escalante was bewildered. He called other students and asked them if anything wrong had happened during the test. They all denied they had copied from other student tests. They said the proctor had watched them throughout the test. Copying could not have happened.

The ETS College Board reexamined the eighteen tests and found that fourteen had answers that closely agreed with the computations of other tests taken in the same room. Fourteen of the eighteen tests were now under a cloud of suspicion. Escalante contacted ETS and pointed out that all eighteen students had been studying together for a long time. It could be expected that their computations would match. Because they worked closely with one another, they would solve problems in a similar way. The officials at ETS were not convinced. They felt sure some copying had taken place.

Jaime Escalante had been planning another trip to Bolivia to visit his mother in La Paz. She was in poor health, and he was anxious to spend some time with her. Now, with this AP class under suspicion, he could not go. His heart aching, Escalante tried to figure out what had happened. He knew how hard his students had studied. He knew they were capable of honestly succeeding in the test. Did the officials at ETS look at the tests with more skepticism than usual because they were all Mexican Americans? Was there a feeling those educators had that minority students from a poor neighborhood simply were in over their heads to even try to pass such a rigorous test?

Jaime Escalante drove to the ETS office in Eagle Rock, near Pasadena. He met with the head of the ETS office in the West. Escalante demanded to see the tests in question where his students had allegedly copied. But he could not. The ETS official assured Escalante that no discrimination based on the ethnic backgrounds of the students had taken place. Escalante looked at the official and said, "Maybe you had a code or something that identified the kids like ours taking the test," adding, "I know well how to spell discrimination."[3] Henry Gradillas was scheduled to meet with Escalante at the ETS office, but Escalante did not wait for him. Later, Escalante explained that it was his, Escalante's and his students fight, and they had to handle it.

A Mexican-American activist in Los Angeles got word of what had happened. He urged Escalante to contact the media and publicize what his students were going through. Escalante feared that the incident would turn into a media circus and harm his students.

Along with the letter accusing the students of cheating, the ETS had offered a solution. If the students whose tests were questioned wanted to take a retest it could be arranged. Many of the students resisted this solution. They argued that it was not fair. Much time had passed since they had studied for the test. They would not be able to do as

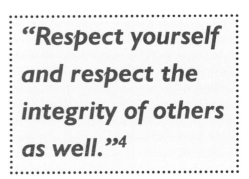

"Respect yourself and respect the integrity of others as well."[4]

well as they had done the first time. Jaime Escalante gathered all his students together. He encouraged them to take the retest. It was the only way to restore their reputation.[5]

Finally, the students agreed with Escalante that they needed to take the retest to keep their own self-respect. Twelve of the fourteen students whose tests were in question arrived for the retest. They had only a weekend to prepare. The students treated the Tuesday test like a once-beaten team treats a rematch. They were eager for the contest. As they were walking to the room they thought about Escalante, their coach, always cheering for the team. The opponent here was not another team—it was the Educational Testing Service. So the students marched to the room chanting, "Beat ETS!"[6]

The proctors in the room placed the students far from one another so there would not be the remotest chance of anyone copying another student's paper. The room grew silent as the tests were passed out. The students thought that this retest was much harder than the original test.

At home, Jaime Escalante paced around, too nervous to do anything else. He knew it was all riding on the outcome of this retest. There were many people who thought from the beginning that Mexican-American students just could not do advanced math. The cheating scandal confirmed their opinions. If the retest failed, those who doubted the students would have won.

On September 13, two weeks after the retest had been sent to ETS, Escalante and the students were still

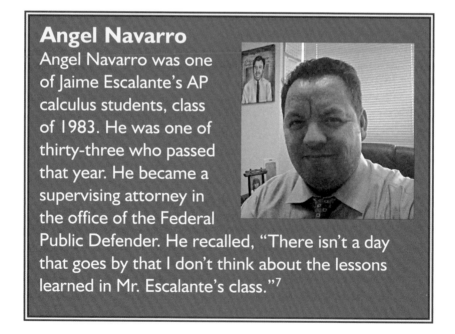

Angel Navarro

Angel Navarro was one of Jaime Escalante's AP calculus students, class of 1983. He was one of thirty-three who passed that year. He became a supervising attorney in the office of the Federal Public Defender. He recalled, "There isn't a day that goes by that I don't think about the lessons learned in Mr. Escalante's class."[7]

waiting for the results. When they could not wait any longer, they called Princeton, New Jersey. The results were given over the phone. Five students earned 5s. Three students earned 4s. There were four 3s. All of the twelve who took the retest had passed. The students were vindicated. Garfield High School was vindicated, and Jaime Escalante became an instant hero.

This mural shows Jaime Escalante (right) with Edward James Olmos, who played Escalante in the movie *Stand and Deliver*. Hector Ponce painted the mural in the Westlake district of Los Angeles.

Fame and Legacy

When news of the student-retest triumph reached the media on September 29, 1982, Jaime Escalante was hailed as a hero. The students who proved they could pass a rigorous AP calculus test were celebrated. It was a heartwarming story of a dedicated teacher and students from a disadvantaged neighborhood winning against a system that often seemed stacked against them. Los Angeles television widely covered the story. From there it went nationwide, exploding into a major story.

In La Paz, Bolivia, Olimpia Escalante de Ortuno listened to the Voice of America, an American station that broadcasts news around the world in the native language of each country. She heard the story of how her brother and his calculus students had overcome accusations of cheating to demonstrate their skill to the world. She called Sara Escalante, their mother, with the news. The family rejoiced that Jaime Escalante had become a hero in the United States.

By the spring of 1983, Jaime Escalante's classroom had become a showcase at Garfield High. The room featured huge color photographs of basketball superstars like Wilt Chamberlain and Jerry West. Posters praised the values of hard work, determination, and discipline.

In August 1983, Escalante returned to Bolivia for a visit with his family. His sisters and brothers were all thriving. Olimpia and Bertha had gone from teachers to school administrators. The brothers were in education and finance. All the family gathered to celebrate Jaime Escalante's success and fame. Sara Escalante proudly showed her son the scrapbook she had been keeping recounting his triumph. Though Sara Escalante's spirit was still strong, it was clear that she was growing weaker. Six months after his visit, Escalante received a phone call from his mother. She told him to be good to his wife and children and she said good-bye. The next day she died in the arms of her daughter, Bertha.

In 1984, Escalante made two trips to Washington, D. C. He attended the Conference of Hispanic Educators, and he met President Ronald Reagan and Mexican president Miguel de la Madrid Hurtadoat at a White House dinner.

In 1987, both the Escalante sons were doing well. Jaimito worked in the electronics and medical technology field. Fernando drove his father's beloved Volkswagen to engineering classes at California State Polytechnic University in Pomona. In that same year, seventy-three students at Garfield High passed the AP

President Ronald Reagan welcomed Escalante at a teacher's lunch in 1984.

calculus test. It was the high point of Escalante's career, but the situation was about to change.

Principal Henry Gradillas, with whom Escalante had good relations, was leaving to pursue his doctorate. Problems grew at Garfield for Escalante.[1] His fame had stirred the jealousies of some fellow teachers. He seemed to be getting too much attention. Literature teacher Carlos Jimenez said, "There are many of us at this school who are knocking themselves out and don't get the attention."[2] Another Garfield teacher, John Bennett said, "I think a lot of people feel Escalante has built a little empire."[3] New principal Maria Elena Tostado tried to minimize the rift between Escalante and his colleagues.[4] One of the reasons why Jaime Escalante got new desk chairs and a bigger classroom was he was teaching more students per hour than any other teacher at Garfield, except for the physical education teachers.

At this time, film producer Tom Musea and director Ramon Menendez contacted Jaime Escalante. Menendez believed the student scores at Garfield would not have been questioned if the students had been Anglos and not Mexican Americans. Musea and Menendez wanted to make a movie about Jaime Escalante and the triumph of his students. Escalante was very busy with his classes and he said, "Go ahead and write it, but I really don't have much time to deal with you."[5] However, Escalante warmed to the idea when Mexican-American actor Edward James Olmos was chosen to play Escalante in the movie to be titled, *Stand and Deliver*.

Jaime Escalante allowed Olmos to spend up to eighteen hours a day with him for a month as he prepared to play him. Olmos attended Escalante's classes, studied his personality, and even gained forty pounds so he would look more like the stocky teacher. "This film is really about the triumph of the human spirit," Olmos said. "It's about something we've lost—the joy of learning, the joy of making our brains develop."[6]

Stand and Deliver was released in 1988 to wonderful reviews. Escalante was very pleased with it. It quickly

Edward James Olmos

Olmos was born in East Los Angeles to parents who had dropped out of school, then struggled to complete their education. Though a good basketball player as a youth, Olmos dreamed of an acting career. He gained bit parts in motion picture and television productions while working at other jobs. Finally, he was cast in a Broadway musical drama *Zoot Suit*. After this, he won major television series roles, including a part on the series *Miami Vice* for which he won an Emmy and a Golden Globe. Olmos was proud to play Jaime Escalante in *Stand and Deliver*.

Actor Edward James Olmos (left) speaks with Jaime Escalante on location at Garfield High School while filming *Stand and Deliver* in 1988.

became a classic, showing what a hardworking and dedicated teacher could achieve and how students could rise far above expectations. In addition to its release in theaters throughout the country, it has been shown many times in schools, libraries, youth camps, and even prisons.

> **"Futures** *is a beautifully crafted series that will have far reaching impact on our nation's youth."[7]*
> *—Admiral James D. Watkins, former secretary of energy.*

In the same year, 1988, *Escalante: The Best Teacher in America* by Jay Mathews was published. Escalante's program of AP calculus continued to thrive at Garfield High, but tensions increased. As famous people like then presidential candidate George Herbert Walker Bush and actor Arnold Schwarzenegger (later governor of California) visited Escalante's classroom, resentments grew. President Ronald Reagan awarded Escalante the Presidential Medal for Excellence in Education. The teacher also received the Hispanic Heritage award for his significant contributions to Hispanic education.

Jaime Escalante lost the math chairmanship at Garfield, and he was receiving hate mail and even death threats from strangers.[8] Beginning in 1990, Escalante worked on a Public Broadcasting Service (PBS) special titled *Futures*. He hosted *Futures I* and *Futures II* over the next several years. The shows demonstrated the practical applications of mathematics in many careers. The programs showed how math plays a role in agriculture, aircraft design, architecture, and automotive design. Famous people like Blue Angel pilots, racecar drivers, and sports personalities were featured. All the episodes illustrated Jaime Escalante's desire to make math fun and meaningful to young people. A segment of *Futures* won the George Foster Peabody Award, the highest honor in broadcasting.

Honorary doctorates from all over the country and even outside the United States were conferred on Jaime Escalante. He was honored by California State University; Concordia University in Montreal, Canada; the University of Northern Colorado; and the University of Massachusetts in Boston. Jaime Escalante had taught at Garfield High School for seventeen years, but in 1991 he quit. Citing differences with his colleagues and a desire for "a change of scenery" as reasons for his resignation, Escalante immediately took another job.[9]

Jaime Escalante was hired by Hiram Johnson High School in Sacramento, California. The school had many different ethnic groups. "Here at Hiram Johnson," Escalante explained, "I have the Anglo kids, the black kids, the Chicano kids, and also the kids from Vietnam, and I have to use a different approach when I talk to each kid."[10] In the prior year, only six students had passed the AP calculus test at Hiram Johnson. Though Escalante remained a hardworking teacher who loved all his students, he did not have the kind of success at his new school that he had enjoyed at Garfield. There were many reasons including the fact that he was now more than sixty years old, and he was more accustomed to dealing with Mexican-American students. He had worked incredibly hard at Garfield High School, and he was tired. In 1998, at the age of sixty-seven, Escalante retired. But he continued to bond with students. He returned to East Los Angeles to speak and the students gathered around him. An observer noted how they "huddled close by him and put their arms around him and called him by his old nickname, Kimo."[11] Escalante was deeply touched and he commented that "to be back here with these kids, to remember the good life back then, it is a real plus."[12]

In 1999, Jaime Escalante was inducted into the National Teachers Hall of Fame. He was honored for a total of thirty-three years in the classroom, twenty-four in the United States, and nine years in Bolivia. Escalante's fame, according to the officials at the Hall of Fame, never distracted him from his underlying purpose, "working to have children believe in their ability to achieve."[13]

After so many years away from family and friends, Jaime Escalante and his wife retired to Bolivia, but he often returns to the United States. The Escalantes live in Cochabamba, and he teaches math part-time at the

Universidad de Valle. He is also available for tutoring at his home. Sometimes Jaime Escalante teaches with his son, Fernando Escalante. They appear at workshops for Bolivian teachers. In Bolivia, Escalante is a well-loved celebrity, but he is as untouched by fame as he was in the United States. He usually wears a brimmed cap and a red sweater over a long-sleeved shirt. His trademark square, tinted glasses are ever present.

Several schools have been named for Jaime Escalante in Bolivia and even a park bears his name. At the dedication of the park, Escalante said to himself, "This is great. Now I'll never be homeless because I'll have a park."[14]

In the years since he retired from Hiram Johnson High School, Escalante has traveled in the United States and all over the world. Escalante came to Capistrano Valley High School in Mission Viejo, California, in February 2006. The gymnasium was filled with chanting teenagers. They called out "Kimo-Kimo," and, as freshman Eden Perez said, "He's like an idol." Cindy Alvarez added, "The stuff that goes on today with us Mexicans with people not believing in us. Other teachers maybe say it, but he really believes in us." The principal of Capistrano Valley, Tom Ressler, marveled, "He's like a rock star."[15]

Jaime Escalante's legacy as a teacher is in the many lives he has touched. The students he taught frequently say they will never forget him. They have gone into many professions and his wise counsel has helped them succeed. Escalante has also touched many more students

The movie *Stand and Deliver* helped spread the legacy of Jaime Escalante's dedication to his students. Above is Edward James Olmos playing Escalante in a scene from the movie.

U.S. Secretary of Education Rod Paige (left) introduces Jaime Escalante on April 17, 2002, at Rancho High School in Las Vegas, Nevada. The two were part of a town meeting that addressed the dropout rate of Latino students.

in his *Futures* series. In the movie *Stand and Deliver*, uncounted thousands have seen the inspirational story of teenagers with little hope for the future lifted up by someone who believed in them.

The Bolivian immigrant who was willing to mop floors on his way to making it in America not only lighted a shining path for other immigrants, but for American-born young people as well. His message is profound but simple—believe in yourself and work hard and you will get there. That is the legacy of Jaime Escalante.

Chronology

1930—Jaime Escalante Gutierrez born in La Paz, Bolivia, on December 31.

1944—Enrolls in Jesuit-run San Calixto High School.

1951—Begins college at Normal Superior teachers' school.

1952—First teaching assignment teaching math at the American Institute.

1954—Graduates from Normal Superior College.

Marries Fabiola Tapia on November 25.

Begins teaching math at San Calixto High School.

1955—Jaime Jr. (Jaimito) born September 27.

1963—Immigrates to the United States, arriving on Christmas Eve.

1964—Begins working at the Van de Kamp restaurant.

Enrolls at Pasadena City College.

1967—Begins work in electronics at Burroughs Corporation.

1969—Second son, Fernando, born July 14.

Graduates from Pasadena City College with Associate of Arts degree.

1973—Receives Bachelor of Arts degree in mathematics from California State University, Los Angeles.

1974—Receives California Teaching Credential.

Begins teaching math at Garfield High School in East Los Angeles.

1978—Begins teaching Advanced Placement (AP) calculus.

1980—Six of nine students pass AP calculus test and receive college credit.

1982—Eighteen students take AP calculus test and pass. Fourteen accused of cheating and offered retest. Twelve take retest and all pass, receiving college credit. Incident propels students and teacher into national prominence.

1988—Story of Escalante and students made into Warner Brothers film—*Stand and Deliver*, a story of triumph of the human spirit.

Jay Mathews biography of Escalante, *Escalante: The Best Teacher* in America, is published.

1990—Begins hosting Public Broadcasting Service (PBS) series—*Futures*—to demonstrate role mathematics plays in many careers.

Series wins George Foster Peabody Award, the highest honor in broadcasting.

Resigns from Garfield High School. Hired by Hiram Johnson High School in Sacramento, California.

1998—Resigns from Hiram Johnson High School. Moves to Cochabamba, Bolivia, with wife; teaches part-time at the Universidad de Valle.

1999—Inducted into National Teachers Hall of Fame.

Chapter Notes

CHAPTER 1. STARTING OVER

1. Alfredo Santana, "Mr. Inspiration," *PCC Spotlight*, p. 1, n.d., <http://www.netaonline.org/ERFUTURE1.htm> (February 6, 2008).
2. Jay Mathews, *Escalante: The Best Teacher in America* (New York: Henry Holt and Company, 1988), p. 55.
3. Jaime Escalante, "Quotes," *Learning to Give*, p. 1, © 2008, <http://www.learningtogive.org/search/quotes/Display_Quotes.asp?author_id=207&search_type=author> (February 6, 2008).

CHAPTER 2. CHILDHOOD IN BOLIVIA

1. Sebastian Rotella, "Taking His Stand to the Homeland: Jaime Escalante," *Los Angeles Times*, June 14, 1999, p. 1.
2. "Excellence: Do It Right the First Time: An Interview With Jaime Escalante," *Center for Digital Government*, p. 1, © 2007, <http://www.centerdigitalgov.com/story.php?id=46880> (February 6, 2008).
3. Jay Mathews, *Escalante: The Best Teacher in America* (New York: Henry Holt and Company, 1988), p. 9.
4. Ibid., p. 27.
5. "Excellence: Do It Right the First Time."
6. Ibid.

CHAPTER 3. A STUDENT AT SAN CALIXTO

1. "'Hero' Teacher Escalante Addresses Students at Wittenberg Commencement," April 13, 2004,

<http://www.4.wittenberg.edu/news/1998/commspeaker.shtml> (October 2007).

2. "Excellence: Do It Right the First Time: An Interview With Jaime Escalante," *Center for Digital Government*, p. 2, © 2007, <http://www.govtech.net/magazine/visions/feb98vision/escalante.php> (February 6, 2008).

3. Jay Mathews, *Escalante: The Best Teacher in America* (New York: Henry Holt and Company, 1988), p. 9.

4. Ibid., p. 31.

CHAPTER 4. TEACHER, HUSBAND, FATHER

1. Carol Novak, "Interview With Jaime Escalante," *Technos Quarterly*, Spring 1993, Vol. 2, No. 1, p. 7, <http://www.ait.net/technos/tq_02/1escalante.php> (October 2007).

2. "Famed Teacher Escalante Talks About His Unique and Successful Philosophy," *Lyon College News Bureau*, September 22, 2006, <http://www.lyon.edu/webdata/groups/Public%20Relations/Escalante%20lecture.htm> (February 6, 2008).

3. Jaime Escalante, "Jaime Escalante Math Program." *The Journal of Negro Education*, Vol. 59, No. 3 (Summer 1990), pp. 407–423. <http://metromath.org/library/uploads/Escalante.pdf> (February 6, 2008).

4. Jay Mathews, *Escalante: The Best Teacher in America* (New York: Henry Holt and Company, 1988), p. 47.

CHAPTER 5. COMING TO CALIFORNIA

1. Jay Mathews, *Escalante: The Best Teacher in America* (New York: Henry Holt and Company, 1988), p. 51.

2. Ibid., p. 52.

3. Alfredo Santana, "Mr. Inspiration," *PPC Spotlight*, p. 1, May 16, 2003, <http://www.pasadena.edu/about/history/alumni/escalante/escalante.cfm> (February 6, 2008).

4. Ibid.

5. Patricia Demchak, "Jaime Escalante Notes Importance of 'Ganas,'" p. 1, *The Baylor Lariat*, October 14, 1998, <http://www.baylor.edu/Lariat/news.php?action-story&story-12545> (October 2007).

6. "Excellence: Do It Right the First Time: An Interview With Jaime Escalante," *Center for Digital Government*, p. 6, © 2007, <http://www.govtech.net/magazine/visions/feb98vision/escalante.php> (October 2007).

7. Santana, p. 1.

Chapter 6. Electronics and Education

1. Alfredo Santana, "Mr. Inspiration," *PPC Spotlight*, p. 2, May 16, 2003, <http://www.pasadena.edu/about/history/alumni/escalante/escalante.cfm> (February 6, 2008).

2. Patricia Demchak, "Jaime Escalante Notes Importance of 'Ganas,'" *The Baylor Lariat*, p. 1, October 14, 1998, <http://www/baylor.edu/Lariat/news.php?action-story&story=12545> (October 2007).

3. Santana, p. 1.

4. *About the National Science Foundation*, n.d., <http://www.nsf.gov/about> (October 2007).

5. Jaime Escalante, *Learning to Give*, p. 1, © 2008, <http://www.learningtogive.org/search/quotes/Display_Quotes.asp?author_id=207&search_type=author> (February 6, 2008).

6. Ron La Brecque, "Something More Than Calculus," *The New York Times*, November 6, 1988, p. A20.

7. "Excellence: Do It Right the First Time: An Interview With Jaime Escalante," *Center for Digital Government*, p.3, © 2007, <http://www.centerdigitalgov.com/story.php?id =46880> (October 2007).

CHAPTER 7. GARFIELD HIGH SCHOOL

1. Kim Hubbard, "Beating Long Odds, Jaime Escalante Stands and Delivers," *People Weekly*, April 11, 1988, Vol. 29, No. 4, p. 57.
2. Ron La Brecque, "Something More Than Calculus," *The New York Times*, November 6, 1988, p. A20.
3. Hubbard, p. 57.
4. La Brecque, p. A20.
5. Carole Novak, "Interview With Jaime Escalante," *Technos Quarterly*, Spring 1993, Vol. 2., No. 1, p. 5, <http://www/ ait/net/technos/tg-02/Escalante.php> (October 2007).
6. Hubbard, p. 57.
7. Maggie Griffin, "To Inspire, Be Inspired," *National Aeronautical and Space Administration*, p. 1, June 29, 2006, <http://www.nasa.gov/audience/foreducators/postsecond ary/features/F_To_Inspire_Be_Inspired.html> (February 6, 2008).
8. La Brecque, p. A20.
9. "Excellence: Do It Right the First Time: An Interview With Jaime Escalante," *Center for Digital Government*, p. 7, © 2007, <http://www.centerdigitalgov.com/story.php?id =46880> (October 2007).
10. Ibid.

Chapter 8. The Advanced Placement Class

1. Carole Novak, "Interview With Jaime Escalante," *Technos Quarterly*, Spring 1993, Vol. 2., No. 1, p. 3, <http://www/ait/net/technos/tg-02/Escalante.php> (October 2007).

2. Sam Dillon, "Advanced Placement Tests Are Leaving Some Behind," *The New York Times*, February 7, 2007, p. B9.

3. Ron La Brecque, "Something More Than Calculus," *The New York Times*, November 6, 1988, p. A. 20.

4. Kim Hubbard, "Beating Long Odds: Jaime Escalante Stands and Delivers," *People Weekly*, April 11, 1988, Vol. 29, No. 14, p. 57.

5. "Famed Teacher Escalante Talks About His Unique and Successful Philosophy," *Lyon College News Bureau*, September 22, 2006, <http://www.lyon.edu/webdata/groups/Public%20Relations/Escalante%20lecture.htm> (February 6, 2008).

6. "Excellence: Do It Right the First Time: An Interview With Jaime Escalante," *Center for Digital Government*, p. 3, © 2007, <http://www.centerdigitalgov.com/story.php?id=46880> (February 6, 2008).

7. Daniel Schugurensky, "Selected Moments of the 20th Century," p. 1, January 19, 2003, <http://www.oise.utoronto.ca/research/edu20/moments/1982escalante.html> (February 6, 2008).

8. Hubbard, p. 57.

CHAPTER 9. A CRISIS IN THE AP CLASS

1. Kim Hubbard, "Beating Long Odds Jaime Escalante Stands and Delivers," *People Weekly*, April 11, 1988, Vol. 29, No. 14, p. 57.
2. Jay Mathews, *Escalante: The Best Teacher in America* (New York: Henry Holt and Company, 1988), p. 138.
3. Ibid., p. 165.
4. Carol Novak, "Interview With Jaime Escalante," *Technos Quarterly*, Spring 1993, Vol. 2, No. 1, p. 6, <http://www/ait/net/technos/tg-02/Escalante/php> (October 2007).
5. Ron La Brecque, "Something More Than Calculus," *The New York Times*, November 6, 1988, p. A20.
6. "Jaime Escalante Math Program," *The Journal of Negro Education*, Vol. 5, No. 3, (Summer 1990), pp. 407–423. See <http://metromath.org/library/uploads/Escalante.pdf> (February 6, 2008).
7. "Jaime Escalante's Students: Where Are They Now?" *The Futures Channel*, p. 1, © 2008, <http://www.thefutures channel.com/jaime_escalante/jaime_escalante_students.php> (October 2007).

CHAPTER 10. FAME AND LEGACY

1. Jerry Jessness, "Stand and Deliver Revisited," p. 4, July 2002, <http://www.reason.com/news/show/28479.html> (October 2007).
2. Kim Hubbard, "Beating Long Odds Jaime Escalante Stands and Delivers," *People Weekly*, April 11, 1988, Vol. 29, No. 14, p. 57.
3. Ron La Brecque, "Something More Than Calculus," *The New York Times*, November 5, 1988, p. A20.
4. Ibid.

5. Hubbard, p. 57.

6. Edward James Olmos, *Hispanic Heritage Biographies*, p. 1, n.d., <http://gale.com/free_resources/chh/bio/olmos_e.htm> (October 2007).

7. "Response to *Futures* With Jaime Escalante," p. 1, n.d., <http://fasenet.org/store/futures/futquotes.htm> (October 2007).

8. Jessness, p. 6.

9. Susan Heller Anderson, "Chronicle," *The New York Times*, p. 1, June 15, 1991, <http://query.nytimes.com/gst/full page.html?res=9D0CE5DB103CF936A25755C0A96795 8260> (October 2007).

10. "Excellence: Do It Right the First Time: An Interview With Jaime Escalante," *Center for Digital Government*, p. 6, © 2007, <http://www.centerdigitalgov.com/story.php?id=46880> (February 6, 2008).

11. James Rainey, "Escalante Again Stands and Delivers," *Los Angeles Times*, November 15, 1998, p. 1.

12. Ibid.

13. "Jaime Escalante, 1999 Inductee," *National Teachers Hall of Fame*, p. 1, n.d., <http://www.nthf.org/inductee/escalante.htm> (October 2007).

14. Sebastian Rotella, "Taking His Stand to Homeland," *Los Angeles Times*, June 14, 1999, p. 1.

15. Hubbard, p. 57.

Further Reading

Alegre, Cèsar. *Extraordinary Hispanic Americans*. New York: Children's Press, 2007.

Kanellos, Nicolàs, Robert Rodriguez and Tamra Orr. *Great Hispanic-Americans*. Lincolnwood, Ill.: Publications International, 2005.

Pateman, Robert and Marcus Cramer. *Bolivia*. New York: Marshall Cavendish Benchmark, 2006.

Pickover, Clifford A. *Calculus and Pizza: A Cookbook for the Hungry Mind*. Hoboken, N.J.: John Wiley, 2003.

Romero, Maritza. *Jaime Escalante: Inspiring Educator*. New York: PowerKids Press, 1997.

Zannos, Susan. *Careers in Science and Medicine*. Bear, Del.: Mitchell Lane Publishers, 2002.

Internet Addresses

FutureChannel.com

Jaime Escalante discusses education and mathematics
<http://www.thefutureschannel.com/jaime_escalante.php>

Futures

Inspiring video of Escalante doing math demonstrations
<http://www.netaonline.org/ERFUTURE1.htm>
<http://www.netaonline.org/ERFUTURE2.htm>

Index